THE YORUBA
OF
SOUTHWESTERN NIGERIA

By

WILLIAM BASCOM

Waveland Press, Inc.
Prospect Heights, Illinois

For information about this book, please write or call:

Waveland Press, Inc.
P.O. Box 400
Prospect Heights, Illinois 60070
(312) 634-0081

Foreword

About the Author

William Bascom was Professor of Anthropology and Director of the Robert
H. Lowie Museum of Anthropology at the University of California, Berkeley. Previously he taught at Northwestern University from 1939 to 1957. He took his B.A. in
physics and his M.A. in anthropology at the University of Wisconsin, and his Ph.D. at
Northwestern University in 1939. He began his studies of the Yoruba in 1937, and has
done fieldwork among the Kiowa of Oklahoma (1935), the Gullah Negroes of Georgia
and South Carolina (1939), on Ponape in Micronesia (1946), and among the "Lucumi"
of Cuba (1948). He is the author of *A Pocket Guide to West Africa* (with Ralph Bunche
and the O.S.S. Staff, 1943), *The Sociological Role of the Yoruba Cult Group* (1944),
Handbook of West African Art (with Paul Gebauer, 1953, 1964), *Ponape: A Pacific
Economy in Transition* (1965), *African Arts* (1967), and *Ifa Divination: Communication between Gods and Men in West Africa* (1969). With Melville J.
Herskovits he edited *Continuity and Change in African Cultures* (1959, 1962), which
has been translated as *Al Thaqafah al Afreequiyyah* (1966).

About the Book

In this case study Professor Bascom presents a picture of the culture of
one of the most interesting and important peoples of Africa. The Yoruba constitute one of the largest ethnic groups south of the Sahara. Their tradition of
urban life makes them unique not only among African societies but among traditionally nonliterate peoples the world over. The Yoruba were also for more than a
century the dominant group among Nigeria's educated elite, providing school
teachers, clerks, and other white collar workers both in Nigeria and in neighboring
territories. In addition the Yoruba are of interest because of the contribution
which the Yoruba slaves and their descendants have made to the culture of the
Caribbean and South America (Brazil and Cuba).

The Yoruba, with other west African groups, represent a high level of
cultural achievement in sub-Saharan Africa. Professor Bascom offers the reader
a detailed description of the elaborate economic, political, and social structures of
the Yoruba, the complex set of religious beliefs, and the world-famous art forms.
The nonspecialist will be impressed as he finds a political organization including
a king, town chiefs, palace chiefs, provincial chiefs, police, body guards, a system
of wards, and an elaborate system of courts. The reader will also find in the traditional Yoruba culture elements similar to installment buying, credit, savings clubs,
and the use of money in the form of cowrie shells, and the practice of "pawning"
one's cocoa trees to be used by a debtor until the debt is paid. The importance of
the profit motive is found also in the formal market system where trading and

bargaining involves credit and the practice of using commissions.

The reader may find the description of the practice of polygamy interesting. A man's several wives seem to be able to live together in close proximity and in relative harmony. One of the mechanisms for integrating a new wife into a compound lay in appointing one of the established wives in the compound as an intermediary and "senior" wife of the fiancé, thus insuring her cooperation. She carried installments of bridewealth to the fiancé's house, carried messages back and forth, and often gave presents of her own to the fiancé. Until she had a child, the bride lived with the "senior wife," who often furnished consolation and support for her.

Also of interest are the male-female roles. The culture would appear to be male-oriented. The wife usually lives in a compound with the groom's father and the kinship system is strongly patrilineal in practice. A wife must not address her husband by personal name or by nickname. If he has a living child, she may address him as "Father of so-and-so," but if not, she cannot use any form of address and must find some expression to catch his attention. While their role may outwardly appear to be subservient in social interaction, women play very important and respected roles in the economic sphere. The complex markets are in the control of women. Some women may merely carry their husband's produce to market and turn over the money to their husbands, but many are professional traders, bargaining with the producer and consumer to obtain as large a margin of profit as possible. Other women traders are commissioned agents who deal regularly with a particular producer. The situation results in many women becoming economically independent, and some possessing more wealth than their husbands.

The author is acutely aware of the problems facing him in writing this book. First he faces the problem of selection and elimination. Since the Yoruba culture is so complex even on the local level, he has tried to avoid elaborate listing of data.

Secondly, Professor Bascom recognizes the danger in generalizing about "the Yoruba." The number and geographical spread of the people has resulted in considerable regional variability. The account is confined mainly to the city of Ifẹ, recording extreme regional variations when necessary.

A third and difficult problem confronting the author is how and when to indicate changes. He is describing the Yoruba as they existed from 1937–1938 with contrasting references made to "former times" (meaning the latter half of the nineteenth century). Descriptions of current events in Nigeria since Biafra's declaration of independence and the resulting civil war are available elsewhere, as are descriptions of modernized Nigeria with its jet airstrips, skyscrapers, and other modern accoutrements. But even with the many contemporary technological and political developments, Nigeria's population is substantially composed of people whose tribal identity is still meaningful. This is true of many other contemporary African nations and gives the understanding of tribal culture a particular significance. Of value to the student involved in studying "man" is this account of the Yoruba culture itself as it existed intact, furnishing a complex charter for the behavior of the Yoruba people at a time when the tribal identity had not been transcended by the larger society. And for both Black and White student readers, this case study demonstrates the dignity and elaborateness of one of the significant African cultural traditions.

LOUISE AND GEORGE SPINDLER

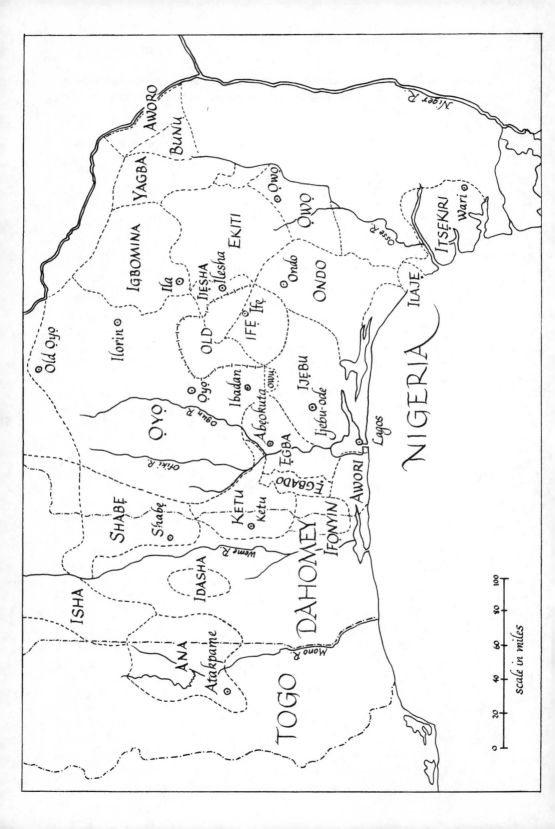

Preface

My fieldwork among the Yoruba began in 1937–1938, when I spent a year working in the city of Ifẹ, except for six weeks in Igana, on a predoctoral fellowship from the Social Science Research Council. During World War II, when I was in government service in West Africa for two and a half years, I revisited Yoruba country many times. In 1950–1951 I returned for another nine months of field work on a Fulbright grant, dividing my time between Mẹko, Ọyọ, and Ilesha, but with visits to many other Yoruba towns. Further research was carried on during a two-month visit when Nigeria received her independence in 1960, and during three months in 1965; these trips were financed by grants from the University of California's Institute of International Studies and the Social Science Research Council. I again express my gratitude to these sponsors, and to the many informants, assistants, officials, and friends in Nigeria who aided me in my work and have helped to make my visits a lasting pleasure to remember.

Three factors, in particular, have made this a difficult book to write. First, Yoruba culture is so complex, even on the local level, that I have had to select, eliminate, condense, and often oversimplify in order to keep within the allotted number of pages. As a result, I fear, what has been included may at times sound like a catalogue, rather than a meaningful description of it; but I see no alternative if any justice is to be given to the richness of Yoruba culture. Books have already been published on Yoruba history, warfare, returned slaves, religion, new churches, cocoa farmers, land law, family property, psychiatric disorder, palaces, proverbs, folktales, and Ijala chanting. In addition to my previous publications on the Yoruba, only a few of which are cited among the recommended readings, I have recently completed a volume on Ifa divination based on research in Ifẹ; and I have material for several volumes based on divination with sixteen cowries at Ọyọ, several other volumes on Yoruba proverbs and myths, and a partially completed monograph on narrow-band weaving at Ọyọ.

Secondly, the sheer number and geographical spread of the Yoruba people has resulted in considerable regional variability. This renders any attempts at generalization dangerous, but at times I have had to speak of "the Yoruba," knowing full well that such statements are likely to be invalid in some areas and, on the local level, for many individuals. I have not attempted to include all that I know of these regional variations because they can be confusing, and because repetitious ascriptions of data to the places where they were recorded can be very boring to nonspecialists, even if there were space to include them. By and large I have confined my account to the city of Ifẹ, both because of its importance to the Yoruba as a whole, and because it was there that I had the opportunity to study the culture most broadly. Nevertheless, on subsequent trips I have learned new things about Yoruba culture, and in several instances I have incorporated this information without having had the opportunity to verify that it actually holds true for Ifẹ.

Thirdly, and perhaps most difficult, has been the attempt to indicate some of the changes that have been taking place in Yoruba culture. They were taking place, certainly, before the nineteenth century with its disruptive warfare, and they have continued since Nigeria became independent. I could have chosen to ignore them and write about a given point in time, say 1937–1938; but this would have meant ignoring change, which is an important feature of culture. Moreover, by that time Yoruba culture had been markedly influenced by the world market and by traders, colonial officials, missionaries, and school teachers. In fact, if their innovations were given the full space that they deserve in describing what the situation was in 1937–1938, little would be left for a discussion of what the Yoruba themselves were like.

Subsequent trips did not allow me sufficient time in Ifẹ to review the changes that have since taken place broadly enough to present an up-to-date picture, and had I been able to do so even less space would have been left for a description of Yoruba culture. In 1937–1938 my informants remembered some details going back to about 1850, but not enough to present a full picture, and the situation was by no means normal at that time. Still other volumes would be required to describe in any detail the many changes that have taken place between that period and my most recent fieldwork in 1965. It has been possible only to mention here some of the differences between Yoruba culture in "former times" or "earlier days" (meaning the latter half of the nineteenth century) and what is happening "now" or "today" (meaning 1937–1938, unless otherwise specified). On the advice of the editors of this series, I have adopted the common anthropological convention of using the "ethnographic present," meaning that I am writing in the present tense about things as they were three decades ago. I hope that readers will not be annoyed by the repetitious use of the above phrases and the resulting changes of tense, or by the use of the present tense for customs some of which may no longer be observed.

A special problem has been raised by Biafra's declaration of independence and the resulting civil war in Nigeria, which continues as I write. I have chosen not to attempt to cover the period since Nigeria's independence, or the events which led up to this war, and to write as if Biafra and the Igbo and other peoples in the Eastern Region are still part of Nigeria, as they were, indeed, during my periods of field research and when the case study of the Igbo was published.

On all these points I ask for the understanding of both my American and Nigerian readers. I am not attempting to present Nigeria as it was at the moment of writing, with its jet airstrips, skyscrapers, and other modern accoutrements, or torn as it is by a civil war, and I would not wish to do so here even if my data permitted it. My primary interest has been to present, as broadly as possible in the space allowed me, an account of the traditional aspects of Yoruba culture, with some indications of the changes that have been taking place. I have tried neither to sensationalize nor to gloss over such elements as human sacrifice, regardless of what the reactions of educated Nigerians, Americans, or Europeans may be; I have enough respect for Yoruba culture as a whole not to be overly concerned about such past customs, particularly when my own country has used atomic bombs and holds the threat of using them again. I can be accused of writing in the present tense of some customs which may have been practiced by only a minority of conservative families in Ife nearly thirty years ago, which may no longer be practiced there, or which even then may not have been customary practices in other parts of Yoruba country; but such is the nature of my data. Criticisms on any of these scores are easily made; I can only say, let anyone do better, and I will welcome their efforts.

The boundaries between Yoruba subgroups on the map by Alex Nicoloff are based largely on my informants' accounts, in which conflicting claims were surprisingly minor. The boundaries of the Ilaje and Itsekiri are based on P. C. Lloyd's "The Itsekiri" (1957) in the Ethnographic Survey of Africa, and boundaries in Togo and Dahomey on M. J. C. Froelich's "Carte des Populations de l'Afrique Noire." The old northern boundary of the kingdom of Ife, before the wars of the last century is shown as —|—|—|—|— .

In 1967 Oyo, Ibadan, Abeokuta, Ijebu, and Ondo Provinces were merged in the Western State, and Ilorin and Kabba Provinces became the West-Central State. The older names are used here, because it is for these units that demographic information is available.

I have departed from conventional Yoruba spelling in using sh instead of ş. I have followed it in using p for kp, ę for ɛ, ǫ for ɔ, and n to represent nasalization except where it appears initially or between two vowels; a, e, i, o, and u have continental values.

WILLIAM BASCOM

Berkeley, California
September 1969

Contents

THE YORUBA
OF
SOUTHWESTERN NIGERIA

The Ọni at his palace in Ifẹ, 1937. Note the beaded cap worn in place of a crown, the beaded cushion and ram's beard fly whisk, the ostrich plumed fan, and the carved house post. Seated at the extreme right is Lowa Ijaruwa, the highest ranking palace chief.

The Alafin of Ọyọ with a son and some of his wives, 1951. Note the beaded crown whose fringes conceal his face, the beaded staff and fly whisk, the embroidered gown, and the hair style worn by his wives.

One of the brass heads from ancient Ifẹ. The lines on the face are completely different from the facial marks used in Ifẹ today. The front of the diadem once had a projection at the top, which has broken away.

Introduction

Importance of the Yoruba

THE YORUBA OF WEST AFRICA are one of the largest ethnic groups south of the Sahara, and in several ways one of the most interesting and important peoples of Africa. If we can place any faith in the population for the Western Region of Nigeria, as reported in the controversial census of 1962, the Yoruba may number 10 or 11 million. Their tradition of urban life gives them a unique place not only among African societies, but among nonliterate peoples the world over. In economics, government, and in particular in art and religion, they rank with those other West African groups which represent the highest level of cultural achievement in sub-Saharan Africa. They are of additional interest because of the contribution which Yoruba slaves and their descendants have made to the culture of the Caribbean and South America, in particular of Cuba and Brazil. The East African slave trade, made famous by Stanley and Livingstone, was in the hands of Arab slavers and fed markets in the Middle East. Nearly all of the slaves brought to the Americas came from West Africa, between Senegal and Angola, and no African group has had greater influence on New World culture than the Yoruba.

Within Nigeria, the Yoruba are one of the three largest and most important ethnic groups. The Hausa, the Igbo, and the Yoruba together constitute more than half of Africa's most populous nation, and they dominate its Northern, Eastern, and Western Regions respectively. For more than a century the Yoruba were the dominant group among Nigeria's educated elite, and they provided school teachers, clerks, and other white-collar workers both in Nigeria and in neighboring territories. Prior to 1937, when Nigeria's first president, Nnamdi Azikiwe, first rose to eminence, they provided political leadership in the development of Nigerian nationalism. Following Nigeria's independence in 1960 they became the minority party when the Hausa and the Igbo formed a coalition, but they still constitute an important element in Nigeria's politics. In terms of economics, which has important political implications, the Yoruba produce nearly all of Nigeria's cocoa, one of the nation's three principal exports.

Population

Bearing in mind that it is already out of date, we must rely on the census of 1952 for most demographic information, since only gross figures were released for the 1962 census. In 1952, 4,114,241 out of a total Yoruba population of 5,248,340, lived in the five provinces which today comprise the Western Region of Nigeria: Ọyọ, Ibadan, Abẹokuta, Ijẹbu, and Ondo. These provinces were overwhelmingly Yoruba, with the percentages of Yoruba in the population ranging from 89.2 percent for Ondo Province to 97.7 percent in Ibadan Province, and with an average of 94.5 percent. These provinces have a combined area of 29,100 square miles, giving an average population density of 150 per square mile, but ranging from a low of 81 in Ọyọ Province to a high of 365 in Ibadan Province. Less than 20 percent of those over seven years of age were literate in the Roman script.

Most of the other Yoruba are found in the Federal Territory (formerly the Colony), in Ilọrin and Kabba Provinces in Northern Nigeria, in Dahomey, and in Togo. In Nigeria the Itsẹkiri of Warri Province are a Yoruba speaking offshoot who have been strongly influenced by Benin. Yoruba traders are found in nearly all the major market towns of West Africa, where they have often been mistaken for Hausa. Descendants of Yoruba slaves, some of whom can still speak the Yoruba language, are found in Sierra Leone where they are known as Aku, in Cuba where they are known as Lucumi, and in Brazil where they are known as Nago.

During the four centuries of the slave trade, when their territory was known as the Slave Coast, untold numbers of Yoruba were carried to the New World, where their descendants still preserve Yoruba traditions, including some which many Yoruba in Nigeria have forgotten. Political structure, clans and lineages, and art have been destroyed and the family system has been altered; but language, mythology and folktales, music and dance, cooking, and religion have been retained with varying degrees of modification. In several parts of the Caribbean and South America, Yoruba religion has been accommodated to Christianity, with Yoruba deities identified with Catholic saints; in Bahia and Havana, especially, Yoruba religion flourishes in an unmistakable form, whereas in Africa it has steadily given way during the past century to both Christianity and Islam. From the Nigerian census of 1952 one can estimate that somewhat more than 40 percent of the Yoruba profess Islam, somewhat less than 40 percent profess Christianity, and less than 20 percent acknowledge allegiance to their traditional religion. Not all of the converts to Christianity and Islam have abandoned the traditional beliefs and rituals, however.

During the first half of the nineteenth century, British ships patrolled the Gulf of Guinea in an effort to suppress the slave trade. The slaves from the slave ships which they captured were freed and set ashore at Freetown, capital of Sierra Leone, where they still constitute a distinct segment of the population. In 1839,

[1] In 1967 the Western Region became the Western State and Ilorin and Kabba Provinces were joined to form the West Central State. The older names are used here because it is for these units that demographic information is available.

300 Yoruba purchased three condemned slave ships and made their way back to Nigeria. They sent back word asking for missionaries from Sierra Leone, opening the way for the first missionaries in Nigeria, who reached the city of Abeokuta in 1842. Among these early missionaries was Samuel Crowther, one of the freed Yoruba slaves, who compiled the first Yoruba Dictionary (1843), and who later became Bishop of the Niger, the first African Bishop of the Church Missionary Society (Anglican) of England. At about the same time, freed slaves began to make their way back from Brazil to Lagos, capital of Nigeria, where their descendants are still distinguished as Aguda, a term also applied to Catholics and to the early Portuguese.

Urbanism

If we exclude the 32,947 Itsekiri, over half of the 5,046,799 Nigerian Yoruba in 1952 lived in cities of over 5000; and over 30 percent lived in cities of over 40,000, of which six were larger than 100,000 including Ibadan, the largest Negro city in Africa. These twelve largest cities, most of which we will be referring to again, were Ibadan, 459,196; Lagos, 276,407; Ogbomosho, 139,535; Oshogbo, 122,728; Ife, 110,790; Iwo, 100,006; Abeokuta, 84,451; Oyo, 72,133; Ilesha, 72,029; Iseyin, 49,680; Ede, 44,808; and Ilorin, 40,994. The Yoruba had an index of urbanization of 39.3, which falls below that of Great Britain with 65.9, Germany with 46.1, and only slightly below the United States with 42.3; but it exceeds Canada with 34.3, France with 31.2, Greece with 25.2, and Poland with 17.4. The Yoruba are the most urban of all African people, and their urban way of life is traditional, dating back well before the period of European penetration.

Ibadan and Abeokuta are not old cities, having been founded in the first half of the last century by refugees from the wars with Ilorin, and Ilorin was only a small village before these wars began. Old Oyo was evacuated and reestablished farther South at the present site during this same period. But of all the Yoruba cities only Lagos, the capital of Nigeria and its principal port and railhead, is comparable to the many new African cities which have developed in recent years at ports, governmental headquarters, and mining centers, as the result of European contact.

The density of some of these cities can be estimated as follows: Abeokuta 5720, Oyo 13,914, Ogbomosho 43,372 (all three in 1931), and Ibadan 55,555 per square mile in 1960. Official estimates of population density are available only for Lagos; 25,000 in 1901, 50,000 in 1921, 58,000 in 1931, and 87,000 in 1950. In 1950 the three wards of Lagos Island had densities of 67,000, 110,000, and 141,000 per square mile. These figures may be compared with those of the four largest cities in the United States in 1960: New York 24,697, Chicago 15,850, Philadelphia 15,743, and Los Angeles 5451.

Yoruba cities are large, and even the traditional ones are dense. Their permanence can be documented by earlier census reports and by estimates going back to 1825, when Yoruba territory was first penetrated by the expedition of Clapperton and Lander. One Yoruba city, Ijebu-Ode, which had a population of

28,000 in 1952, is mentioned repeatedly from 1507–1508 onward and first appears on a Portuguese map of about 1500. It is surrounded by an enormous, ancient earth rampart, 80 miles long, which surrounds the city at distances from about 5 to 15 miles and encloses an area of 400 square miles. It is formed by a bank which is still 15 to 20 feet high and 50 feet wide at the base, and a ditch 20 to 25 feet deep and 40 feet wide, which together create a wall 40 feet high.

Even earlier, before Columbus discovered America, when Portuguese explorers first reached Benin in 1485, they learned of a great king who is almost certainly the Qni of Ifẹ. Word of this king, whom they took to be Prester John, spurred on their exploration of the African coast. Archeological excavations at Ifẹ and at old Qyọ suggest the size and confirm the antiquity of these cities.

The old, traditional cities are farming centers surrounded by belts of farms extending as much as 15 miles outside. Unlike the residents of modern American suburbia and exurbia, the Yoruba commute regularly from their homes in the city to their farms on the periphery; often they stay in their farm huts for weeks at a time when the farming season is at its peak.

The Country

The rhythm of farm work varies with the seasons, which consist of a marked dry season from December through February and a rainy season from April through October. The intervening months are intermediate and variable, and the heaviest rainfall is in June, July, and September. The seasons become more marked and humidity diminishes as one goes inland. Rainfall averages between 40 and 60 inches for most of Yoruba territory, but between 60 and 80 inches for Ijẹbu and the southern part of Ondo Province. Variation in temperature increases as one moves north from the coast with a mean of about 79°, a maximum of 95°, and a minimum of 60° for Lagos; and a mean of about 85°, a maximum of 102°, and a minimum of 50° for Ibadan. During the rainy season the prevailing winds blow inland from the Gulf of Guinea; during the dry season dry, dust-laden harmattan winds blow southward from the Sahara.

Along the coast there are swamp forests, behind which lie the rain forest, the deciduous forests, the Savannah forests, and the Savannah grasslands. Yoruba country is low lying, mostly under 1600 feet above sea level, with a gradual increase in elevation as one moves northward. It extended inland to the River Niger, known in Yoruba as Odo Qya or River Qya, until the city of Old Qyọ was deserted in the nineteenth century. The six other main rivers, Yewa, Ogun, Qmi, Qshun, Shasha, and Qni, flow southward, cutting across the five vegetation zones and emptying into the lagoon, which is separated from the ocean by a narrow and almost continuous sand bar. The lagoon system runs from Dahomey eastward to the Benin River where it connects with the intricate network of creeks of the Niger Delta. It provides an inland waterway for canoes and small craft, and an east-west trade route.

West Africa has its share of tropical diseases, including filariasis, bilharzia, elephantiasis, yaws, sleeping sickness, dysentery, yellow fever, malaria, and blackwater fever. In the days of exploration, malaria seems to have been the principal cause of the high mortality which earned for the Guinea Coast the name of the "White Man's Grave." Among other things this deterred settlement of the region by white colonists, simplifying the transition to independence; but these and other diseases remain important factors in Yoruba life.

Yoruba Subgroups

The name Yoruba has become generally accepted through its early usage in the mission schools, but it was originally given to the Ọyọ Yoruba by the Fulani or the Hausa, and is said to mean "cunning." In 1864, Koelle argued that the missionaries were erring in applying the name to the Yoruba as a whole because the Yoruba had never used it in this way, because it would confuse the Ọyọ with the larger Yoruba cultural and linguistic group, and because the Yoruba themselves would never accept it. Originally there was no comprehensive name for the Yoruba as a whole, and people referred to themselves by the name of their subgroup. The largest of these were the Ọyọ, sometimes referred to as "The Yoruba proper," and in some areas old men still deny that they are Yoruba since they belong to different subgroups.

Starting in the west, the subgroups include the Ana (Ifẹ) and Isha (including the Manigri) astride the Togo-Dahomey boundary; the Idasha (Dassa), an enclave in Dahomey; the Shabẹ (Ishabẹ, Shavẹ), Ketu (Iketu), and Ifọnyin (Ọhọri, Ahori, Holli, Nago, Anago, Dje) astride the Dahomey-Nigeria boundary; the Awori, Ẹgbado, and Ẹgba of Abẹokuta Province and the Federal District; the Ijẹbu (Jẹbu) of Ijẹbu Province and the Federal District; the Ọyọ of Ọyọ, Ilọrin, and Ibadan Provinces; the Ifẹ and Ijẹsha (Jẹsha) of Ọyọ Province; the Ondo, Ọwọ, Ilajẹ, and Ekiti of Ondo Province; the Igbomina of Ilọrin Province; the Yagba, Bunu, and Aworo (Kakanda) of Kabba Province; and the related Itsẹkiri mentioned earlier. Another subgroup, the Owu, whose capital was formerly located between Ifẹ and Ijẹbu Ode, was defeated during the wars of the last century; they took refuge in Abẹokuta where they have merged with and have been partially absorbed by the Ẹgba. These subdivisions do not coincide with either contemporary or traditional political boundaries, but they are related in varying degree to both.

The Ekiti were composed of a number of autonomous kingdoms which joined in a confederacy against the powerful armies of Ibadan in the last century; the people accept both the general name Ekiti and the specific names of these kingdoms, such as Ẹfọn, Ara, Ido, and Ado. In general usage the term Ijẹbu includes the Irẹmọ, who maintain that they are distinct. The Ọyọ, who are the most numerous, recognize six subdivisions grouped into a Right District or Ẹkun Ọtun in the West (comprising the northern Ẹkun Ọtun proper, the central Onko, and the southern Ibarapa) and a Left District or Ẹkun Osi in the East (comprising the northern Ẹkun Osi proper, the central Ibọlọ, and the southern Epo). Anago or Nago, which refers to one specific Yoruba subgroup (Ifọnyin), is also used in Dahomey as a general name for all Yoruba speaking peoples, as it is also in Brazil. The Cuban name Lucumi comes from a Yoruba greeting meaning "My friend"

(Oluku mi), and the Sierra Leone name Aku also comes from the many Yoruba greetings which begin with the root "Ẹku."

Writers have often said that the Yoruba were united under the King of Ọyọ until the wars with Ilọrin during the last century fragmented his kingdom, but there is no evidence to support this claim. It appears to be due to a failure to recognize that early writers referred only to the Ọyọ when they spoke of the Yoruba, to the Ọyọ version of *The History of Yoruba* as presented by Samuel Johnson, and to the ambitions of a colonial official who was stationed in Ọyọ early in this century. When Old Ọyọ was first visited in 1826, Clapperton recorded that the kingdom was bounded by Ketu, Ijẹbu, and Akurẹ in Ondo Province, and extended from 10° north to within 5 miles of the sea near Badagry; even this is an exaggeration according to informants, including those in the court of the King of Ọyọ. At that time Ọyọ was still the largest and most powerful of the Yoruba kingdoms, but if any king outranked the others it was the Ọni of Ifẹ by virtue of his seniority. Letters written to the Ọni by other Yoruba kings in the 1920s and 1930s addressed him as "Father" and were signed "Son," and he replied reciprocally; even Johnson (1921:45) admits that the King of Ọyọ receives his "Sword of Justice" from Ifẹ, "without which he can have no authority to order an execution." Nevertheless the Ọni was only *primus inter pares,* and each kingdom was basically autonomous.

Nor did the various subgroups unite in time of war. Alliances between them were common, but there were also alliances with alien peoples for attacks on other Yoruba groups. The Yoruba do not constitute a "tribe" in a political sense, nor are they comparable to North American Indian tribes. For this reason the word tribe is avoided here, and the Yoruba are spoken of as a people or an ethnic group. There is dialectical variation in the Yoruba language, so that a man from Ọwọ has difficulty understanding a Ketu man at first, and there is considerable local variation in customs and institutions; but there is sufficient underlying cultural and linguistic unity to consider them as a single ethnic group, large and diverse as it may be.

2

Origins and History

Ancient Ifẹ

THERE HAS BEEN MUCH SPECULATION about the origins of the Yoruba people, heightened by the discovery of the now famous Ifẹ brass castings and terra-cottas, and more recently by Nigerian independence. The technically perfect and extremely lifelike and sensitive cast brass heads from Ifẹ— some life-sized—were so different from all other traditional African art that they were bound to raise questions about their origin and about that of the ancestors of the Yoruba.

Leo Frobenius, who first reported these great works of art, held that Yoruba culture had been introduced by Etruscans who reached West Africa by way of the "lost continent" of Atlantis. Sir Flinders Petrie, noting the resemblance of these heads to pottery ones from Memphis, suggested an Egyptian origin; this view has been followed by Talbot and other colonial officials and by many educated Yoruba. Archdeacon J. Olumide Lucas attempted to prove that it derives from Egypt, using unsound linguistic evidence.[1] Dr. Saburi O. Biobaku saw the ancient kingdoms of Meroe in the eastern Sudan as the source of the Yoruba. Earlier writers had noted similarities to Jewish customs, one identifying Yoruba as one of the ten "lost tribes" of Israel. Yoruba converts to Islam generally acclaim Mecca as their point of origin.

Archeology, which is still in its infancy in Nigeria, has not yet provided the answer to these questions. It has established that Ifẹ was the center of an important glass-making industry which may have spread blue glass beads (ṣẹgi, akori) across West Africa. It has unearthed shrine floors paved with potsherds trimmed and set on edge in straight rows, circles, and herringbone patterns. The discovery of full figures cast in brass in 1957, with the size of the head exaggerated in proportion to the body, disposed of speculations that the Ifẹ brasses were the work of errant European or Egyptian artists, or that they had been carried to Ifẹ

---

[1] J. Olumide Lucas, *The Religion of the Yorubas.* Lagos: C. M. S. Bookshop, 1948.

7

during the migration of the Yoruba from a distant point of origin. Nor do serious scholars any longer hold that the art of brass casting, using the lost wax (*cire perdue*) process, was first introduced to Ifẹ and Benin by the Portuguese. As Sir Flinders Petrie first observed, the facial features of these heads and figures resemble those of the inhabitants of Ifẹ today.

Carved figures, stools, and monoliths in granite and quartz, which have been known for over half a century, are believed to date from the "classical period" of Ifẹ when the brasses and terra-cottas were produced. A town wall about 5½ miles in circumference which surrounded the city probably dates from the same period; a second town wall of nearly 8 miles was constructed during the period of the slave wars, probably in the second quarter of the nineteenth century. It is clear that Ifẹ was an artistic and ritual center of great importance during the classical period, which is tentatively dated at 950–1400 A.D. or earlier. As far as Yoruba origins are concerned, the most that archeology has been able to contribute so far is to uncover some stylistic similarities between some Ifẹ terra-cottas and the Nok terra-cottas from Northern Nigeria, which are dated 900 B.C.–200 A.D. Iron and brass are present in these early Nok finds.

Linguistic Evidence

The linguistic evidence indicates, if anything, a western origin of the Yoruba, which is probably the case for most Nigerian languages except Hausa, Kanuri, and other Chad and Saharan languages, whose linguistic affiliations lie to the north and east. All other Nigerian languages, including Yoruba, belong to the Niger-Congo branch of the great Congo-Kordofanian language family which includes most West African languages.[2] Chamba, Vere, Mumuye, Longuda, and Yungur belong to the Adamawa branch of Niger-Congo, which stretches far to the east, also suggesting an eastern origin. Afo, Birom, Tiv, Jukun, Ibibio and other Nigerian languages belong to the Benue-Congo branch which includes Bantu; some of these languages may have spread northward and westward for short distances, but the general direction of movement of this group was toward the east.

The language of the Fulani is related to Serer, Wolof, and other West Atlantic languages, and the eastward movement of the Fulani can be traced historically. The Bargu (Bariba) language is related to Mosi, Grusi, Lobi, Dogon, Senufo, and other languages of the Voltaic branch of Niger-Congo, which, like Fulani, extends westward into upper Volta and Mali. Busa belongs to the Mande branch, which extends westward to Guinea and Sierra Leone. Yoruba belongs to the Kwa branch, which includes Igbo, Ijọ, Edo, Idoma, Igala, Igbira, Gbari, and Nupe, and extends westward through the Ewe, Gan, and Akan to the Kru and Bassa of Liberia. This distribution suggests that if the Yoruba came from the east it was from not much beyond the Niger and that the probability is considerably

---

[2] Joseph H. Greenberg, *The Languages of Africa*, International Journal of American Linguistics, XXIX:1, 1963.

greater that, if they migrated from anywhere, their direction of movement was also from west to east.

Migration Legends and the Creation Myth

The migration legends which are often cited point to the origin of the Yoruba in the very opposite direction. One of these which is common among the peoples of northern Nigeria tells of Kisra, a magician king who came into that area from the East, with one branch moving into Yoruba territory. Another account comes from a copy dated 1824 of part of a document written by Mohammed Bello, Sultan of Sokoto, and presumably based on Hausa verbal tradition. This says that it is supposed that the Yoruba "originated from the remnants of the children of Canaan, who were of the tribe of Nimrod" but who were driven out of Arabia by a prince, Yaa-rooba, and migrated to their present territory leaving some of their people behind wherever they stopped on the way. "Thus it is supposed that all the tribes of Soodan, who inhabit the mountains, are originated from them." Neither of these accounts, however, have been recorded among the Yoruba, although they have sometimes been cited by Yoruba writers.

A third legend, which Samuel Johnson says he recorded from the traditional historians of Ọyọ says that Oduduwa, a son of King Lamurudu of Mecca, reverted to idolatry and was expelled by the faithful Muslims; wandering eastwards from Mecca for ninety days, Oduduwa settled at Ifẹ. Even disregarding the fact that Ifẹ is west of Mecca, no subsequent writer has recorded this legend among the Yoruba.

Conceivably some ancestors of the Yoruba may have come from far to the east, or elsewhere, and adopted a Kwa language from the people among whom they settled; but if these migrants adopted a new language and a new culture, and were physically absorbed by their new neighbors, are they or are the original inhabitants to be considered the ancestors of the Yoruba? Linguistically, culturally, and physically, the peoples most closely related to the Yoruba are their neighbors in the forest belt of West Africa. Some writers have maintained that these myths account only for the origin of the ruling clan, but the Hausa have not become known as Fulani because they have Fulani rulers, nor are the people of Benin known as Yoruba because they acknowledge that their ruling dynasty came from Ifẹ.

The Yoruba's own version of the origin is charmingly ethnocentric. Not only did they originate at the city of Ifẹ, but the earth and the first human beings were created there. This origin myth is widely known and has been recorded in many different variants; it was referred to briefly by Richard and John Lander on May 15, 1830 and published in a fuller version by Samuel Crowther thirteen years later.[3]

According to this myth, as it is told at Ifẹ, the deities originally lived in

---

[3] Samuel Ajayi Crowther, *Vocabulary of the Yoruba Language*. London: Church Missionary Society, 1843.

the sky, below which there was only primeval water. Olorun (Olodumare), the Sky God, gave to Orishala, the God of Whiteness, a chain, a bit of earth in a snail shell, and a five-toed chicken, and told him to go down and create the earth. However, as he approached the gate of heaven he saw some deities having a party, and he stopped to greet them. They offered him palm wine and he drank too much and fell asleep, intoxicated. Odua (Oduduwa), his younger brother, had overheard Olorun's instructions, and when he saw Orishala sleeping, he took the materials and went to the edge of heaven, accompanied by Chameleon. Here he let down the chain and they climbed down it. Odua threw the piece of earth on the water, and placed the five-toed chicken upon it. The chicken began to scratch the earth, spreading it in all directions, and as far as the ends of the earth. After Chameleon had tested the firmness of the earth, Odua stepped on it at Idio where he made his home, and where his sacred grove in Ife is located today.

When Orishala awoke and found that the work had been completed, he put a taboo on wine from the oil palm which his worshipers observe today. He came down to earth and claimed it as his own because he had been sent by Olorun to create and rule it and, as Odua's elder brother, by right of seniority. Odua insisted that he was the owner of the earth because he had made it. The two brothers began to fight and the other deities who followed them to earth took sides with them. When Olorun heard of the fighting, he called Orishala and Odua to appear before him in heaven, and each told his version of what had happened. Olorun said that the fighting should stop. To Odua, Creator of the Earth, he gave the right to own the earth and rule over it, and he became the first King of Ife. To Orishala he gave a special title and the power to mould human bodies, and he became the Creator of Mankind. Olorun then sent them back to earth with Oramfe, the Ife God of Thunder, to keep peace between them, and with Ifa, the God of Divination, and Eleshije, the Ife God of Medicine, as his companions.

This myth points to a local origin not only of the Yoruba but of all mankind. Obviously it does not settle the question of Yoruba origins, but it is important because of the validation it provides for many elements of Yoruba custom and belief. In its many variants it explains the following: why Orishala tabooed wine from the oil palm to his worshipers; why drums are not used in the worship of Odua; the meaning of the names of several deities; the origins of certain songs, proverbs, and greetings or passwords; the origin of the incest taboo and the ritual atonement performed when this taboo is broken; the origin of the quarters and markets of Ife; and the meaning of the full name of Ife (Ile-Ife) as Earth Spreading. The variants differ primarily in the order in which the deities descended from heaven, with narrators claiming greater seniority for their own deity and thus for themselves and their lineage, some variants naming deities other than Odua as Creator of the Earth. Costumed dancers annually commemorate the creation of the earth in Ife rituals, dressed like chickens and dancing as if scratching the earth, and each year at the festival for Odua a five-toed chicken must be sacrificed for the Oni, presented to him by the third ranking town chief, Obaloran.

Most important, this myth provides the charter for the Yoruba people, providing them with a sense of unity through a common origin; because all

Yoruba people claim an ultimate descent from Odua, or Oduduwa, and the Yoruba kings validate their right to rule by claiming lineal descent from him through one of his sixteen sons. The continuing importance of this myth in politics is demonstrated by the founding of the Society of the Children of Odua (Egbe Omo Oduduwa) in 1948 "to unite the various clans in Yorubaland," and its association with the Action Group, a political party which was established three years later.

The Sons of Odua

Yoruba mythology goes on to explain that when Odua grew old he became blind. He sent each of his sixteen sons in turn to the ocean for salt water which had been prescribed as a remedy. Each returned unsuccessfully, bringing only fresh water, until Obokun, the youngest, finally succeeded. Odua washed his eyes in the salt water and could see again. Then he learned that his other sons except Obokun and the Oni, who later succeeded him, had stolen his property and all his crowns except the one he himself wore. In gratitude to Obokun, who became the Owa, or King of Ilesha, he gave a sword; Obokun took it and cut some of the beaded fringes from Odua's crown, and because of this he is not permitted to wear a crown which covers his face, as the other Yoruba kings do. Obokun went to Ilesha where he became king of the Ijesha, and the other sons founded kingdoms of their own.

There are many variants on this Ife myth also, and considerable disagreement from one part of Yoruba territory to another as to which kings of Yoruba territory are the direct descendants of the sixteen sons of Odua. Among the most commonly mentioned are the Oni of Ife, the Alafin of Oyo, the Onishabe of Shabe, the Alaketu of Ketu, the Oshemowe of Ondo, the Owa of Ilesha, the Orangun of Ila, and a number of Ekiti kings including the Alaye of Efon, the Alara of Ara, the Olojudo of Ido, and the Elekole of Ikole. Many include the Oba of Ado, or King of Benin, the Onipopo, or king of the Egun or Popo at Allada and the Onidada, or king of the Fon at Abomey in Dahomey, and the Oninana, or king of the Gan at Accra in Ghana. The Ijesha or people of Ilesha maintain that the Oni himself was not one of the sixteen sons, but the child of a slave left by them to tend Odua's shrine. Like the creation myth, this myth validates the authority of the kings and provides the basis for distinctions in rank between them.

In 1903 the Oni of Ife visited Lagos at the invitation of the Governor to settle the question of whether or not the Elepe of Epe had the right to wear a beaded crown. Ruling the Elepe's claim to be invalid, the Oni went on to list twenty-one kings "to whom crowns have been given by the Oni of Ife": Alake of Abeokuta, Olowu of Owu, Alagura of Gbagura, and Oloko of Oko (all four now at Abeokuta); Alaketu of Ketu, Alafin of Oyo, Akarigbo of Ijebu Remo, Awujale of Ijebu Ode, Oshemowe of Ondo, Olowo of Owo, Oba of Ado (Benin), Owa of Ilesha, Orangun of Ila, Olosi of Osi, and seven Ekiti kings: Ore of Otun, Olojudo of Ido, Ajero of Ijero, Alara of Ara, Elekole of Ikole, Alaye of Efon, and Ewi of Ado Ekiti. In 1917 Governor MacGregor listed these twenty-one kings, including the Oni of Ife but omitting Olowo of Owo, as the only kings permitted to wear beaded crowns and reserving to himself the prerogative to grant titles and the right to wear a crown.

Today there are over fifty "kings" who claim to be descendants of the sons or grandsons of Odua and to have migrated directly from Ifẹ; there are over a hundred kings in all, the remainder having been granted the right to wear beaded crowns by other Yoruba kings. Some of these assumed this status during the last century when the country was torn by warfare; others have done so under Pax Brittanica. Formerly if a town chief (Balẹ) were to wear a beaded crown without the permission of the king (Ọba) to whom he was subject, it was tantamount to an act of treason and the king's armies would have been sent against him. Recently many town chiefs have been granted the right to wear beaded crowns in return for payment or other favors. It is not possible to determine how many kingdoms there actually were before the wars of the last century began, but they probably numbered over twenty.

The Yoruba–Dahomey Wars, 1698–1892

Aside from the early Portuguese references to the Ọni of Ifẹ and to the city of Ijẹbu Ode, recorded history begins with an account of Ọyọ's cavalry invading the kingdom of Allada in southern Dahomey in 1698. By this time the wars which fed the slave trade were well underway, and Yoruba slaves were already being exported from Whydah. Ọyọ, the largest and most powerful of the Yoruba kingdoms, sent its cavalry against the Fọn kingdom of Dahomey in 1724 and 1728, and, as a result, the King of Dahomey began to pay annual tribute to the Alafin, King of Ọyọ. With some interruptions, which brought the Ọyọ armies again and again into Dahomey, this tribute was continued for a century (1729–1827), during which Ọyọ on several occasions interfered with the internal and external affairs of Dahomey. Allada was also paying tribute to Ọyọ, perhaps since its defeat in 1698.

In 1789 Dahomey attacked the capital of the Yoruba kingdom of Ketu, killing many and bringing back 2000 captives. In 1827, when Ọyọ was involved in the Ilọrin wars, the King of Dahomey seized his opportunity and ended the payment of tribute. As the Yoruba became increasingly involved in the Ilọrin wars and in the internal wars between Yoruba states, the annual Dahomean slave wars were frequently directed at Yoruba towns and cities in the Ẹgbado, Ẹgba, Ketu, Shabẹ, Ana, and Ọyọ kingdoms. The growing Ẹgba city of Abẹokuta became a prize target, but expeditions against it failed in 1851, 1861, 1864, 1873, and 1875. Informants old enough to remember these wars spoke with respect of the bravery and ferocity of the Dahomean women warriors who formed part of their army. Bowen, the first American missionary in Nigeria, who travelled through parts of Yoruba territory from 1850 to 1856, described the destruction wrought by the Dahomean and Ilọrin wars, noting that of all the places visited by the Lander brothers in 1830, only three towns and a few villages remained. The wars with Dahomey did not end until its armies were defeated by French forces in 1892.

The Internal Wars, 1817–1893

The end of the previous century had seen Ọyọ enjoying the long rule of Alafin Abiọdun, famed for its peace and prosperity, and the kingdom was at the peak of its power. But things were happening in the north which were to have a profound effect on Yoruba history. The Fulani, who had moved into Nigeria from the west as peaceful nomadic herders, began a Jihad or religious war under the leadership of a Mallam named Usuman dan Fodio. In 1804–1810 the Fulani conquered the Hausa and afterward the Nupe, who are the immediate neighbors of the Yoruba to the north.

Alafin Abiọdun's successor, Arogangan, saw his nephew and war chief, Afọnja of Ilọrin, as a serious rival and, seeking to dispose of him, ordered him to attack a town reputed to be impregnable. Knowing that he must conquer it within three months or die, Afọnja and his lieutenants mutinied in 1817, massacring the Alafin's representatives, besieging Ọyọ, and forcing Arogangan to commit suicide. Afọnja declared Ilọrin independent of Ọyọ and invited Alimi, another Fulani Mallam to join him. Through Alimi, Afọnja encouraged bands of Fulani and Hausa warriors to come to Ilọrin, and they were joined by Hausa slaves of the Alafin who revolted and escaped. Together with increasing numbers of converted Yoruba, they began raiding nearby Yoruba towns and selling their captives into slavery. Samuel Crowther was captured in 1821.

In 1825 Captain Clapperton and Richard Lander explored Yoruba territory, noting a number of burned and deserted villages between Shaki and Ọyọ which had been destroyed by the Fulani and Hausa. Remaining in Ọyọ from January to March 1826, they reported that many Ọyọ were deserting their villages to move south into the forests, but that the large city of Ọyọ was still a stronghold, surrounded by a dry moat and mud wall 15 miles in circumference. Richard and John Lander, revisiting Ọyọ in May 1830, saw even more ruined towns and villages, pillaged by the Fulani. Ilọrin, a prodigious town, had already surpassed Ọyọ in size. They were struck by the ominous changes which had occurred, and practically foretold the fall of Old Ọyọ, or Katunga as they knew it. At that time Ọyọ was located about 80 miles north of the present city of Ọyọ, roughly half way between Jebba on the Niger and Kishi.

In 1831 Afọnja was killed by the bands of raiders he had helped to create, and in the same year Alimi died. The rule of Ilọrin passed to Alimi's ambitious son, Abdul Salami, the first of Ilọrin's dynasty of Fulani Emirs. Ọyọ made attacks on Ilọrin in an attempt to check her power, but they were destined to fail because of internal rivalry, dissension, and outright treachery, which were exploited by the Fulani to their own advantage. Finally, after defeating the Ilọrin armies in 1834 and in 1838, Alafin Oluewu was betrayed and killed in battle and Old Ọyọ was deserted, probably in 1839.[4] Atiba, the next Alafin, established his capital at Ago-ọja, which became the new Ọyọ.

---

[4] For these dates I rely on the diary of Samuel Crowther of September 27, 1841. *Journals of the Rev. James Frederick Schön and Mr. Samuel Crowther, who, with the sanction of her Majesty's Government, accompanied the Expedition up the Niger, in 1841, in behalf of the*

Here the events of Yoruba history become even more complicated by warfare and one must rely on verbal tradition, bearing in mind that some dates may be only approximations and that accounts differ from one faction to another. The conflicts which ensued are verified from a variety of sources, verbal and documentary, but they can be presented here only in a highly oversimplified form. Books have been written on the Yoruba wars of the last century.

Meanwhile the Ifẹ and Ijẹbu had joined forces, strengthened by refugees from Ọyọ towns, and destroyed Owu, a large and highly fortified town after a siege of five or more years. It is said that the dry moat surrounding the town wall was so deep that two palm trees, one on top of the other, would not reach the top. Yoruba authorities put the beginning of the Owu war in 1821; Ifẹ tradition places the fall of Owu during the reign of the Ọni Abeweila, adding that it was made possible by inside information that Abeweila obtained from his mother, who was an Owu. The Ifẹ soldiers used crossbows with poisoned arrows.

The victorious armies pursued Owu survivors into Ẹgba territory, destroying Ẹgba villages, and around 1829 they encamped in Ibadan, a deserted Ẹgba village. The Ẹgba refugees moved south to found the city of Abẹokuta in 1830, where they were joined by refugees from Owu. Refugees from Ọyọ villages rapidly built Ibadan into a gigantic armed camp which became the major force in the ensuing wars. When Ilọrin laid siege for a third time to Oshogbo, in the early 1840s, the Ibadan army came to the rescue and the Ilọrin army was decisively defeated, breaking its power but not ending its attacks on other Yoruba towns.

Other Ọyọ refugees settled in Ifẹ, living in Ifẹ compounds scattered through town and paying fees for the use of farmland. Shortly before his death in 1849, the Ọni Abeweila assigned them land to build their own homes at Modakeke, a site within the town walls of Ifẹ. Abeweila is remembered as a tyrant whose servants hawked ochra and stew leaves about town at exorbitant prices. When a customer called them, they would ask a penny for leaves worth three hundredths of a penny. If the customer refused to pay they would put down their loads and tell Abeweila; then the customer would be lucky if he got off with the payment of £5 or £10. Because of this he was called "One who has very big ochra leaves" (A-bi-ewe-ila bẹrẹngẹdẹ).

Abeweila was succeeded by Kumbushu, who ruled from 1849 to 1878. He is also remembered as a bad ruler because he did nothing to stop his servants, the most notorious of whom was Etitan, from exploiting his subjects. A year after he became Ọni, war broke out between Ifẹ and Modakeke; Ifẹ was defeated and its inhabitants fled 7 miles south to Ishọya where they remained until 1854. It was from this flight that Kumbushu received the name Ogbadegodi, meaning "He took his crown and climbed the town wall" (O-gba-ade-gun-odi).

By this time Dane guns were increasingly available and the Yoruba states were engaged in a costly series of fratricidal wars which continued to the end of the century. Ilọrin conquered Ekiti and attacked other Yoruba areas in the northeast. Ibadan reconquered Ekiti and conquered Ilesha, fought on the south with the

Church Missionary Society. London: Hatchard and Son, Nisbet and Co., 1842. Pp. 317–318. Other dates have been given for these events, but Crowther's were recorded closest to the time when they happened.

Ẹgba, and raided for slaves among the distant Yagba and Bunu as well as within the Ọyọ kingdom itself. In 1862 Ibadan destroyed the large Ọyọ city of Ijaye. The Ẹgba, who were still defending themselves against the repeated attacks by Dahomey, became involved in a succession of wars with Ibadan and with the Ijẹbu, Ẹgbado, and Awori.

These wars culminated in a sixteen year war (1877–1893) in which many of the Yoruba subgroups were involved in battles with Ibadan, which had only the support of Ọyọ. Ibadan was fighting with the Ẹgba and Ijẹbu on the south, with Ifẹ and contingents of Ijẹbu, Ijẹsha, and Ekiti in defense of Modakẹkẹ, with Ilọrin supported by Fulani and Hausa in defense of Ọfa, and at a mammoth war camp known as Kiriji in the east. At Kiriji the Ibadan forces faced the Ekiti, who had reasserted their independence and formed a confederacy by 1879, and whose allies included the Ijẹsha, Igbomina, Ifẹ, Ijẹbu, contingents of Yagba, and the Ilọrin at Ọfa.

At Ifẹ Kumbushu was succeeded by Ọjaja, also known as Ayikiti, who ruled from 1878 to 1881. When Ọjaja died, Derin Ọlọgbẹnla was asked to become Ọni, but he refused. While people were still arguing about what to do about this, the Ifẹ were again driven to Ishọya and nearby towns by Modakẹkẹ. Yoruba country was torn by warfare, and during the entire stay at Ishọya, from 1881 to 1894, the people of Ifẹ had no king. In 1892, while they were still in exile, they saw their first English shilling and the first white man visited Ifẹ, following the defeat of Ijẹbu Ode by government troops from Lagos. During the interregnum, chief Ọruntọ (or Ọbalufẹ) acted as regent and Derin Ọlọgbẹnla signed letters and treaties as "Ọni Elect." Both signed the treaty ending the fighting at Kiriji in 1886, in which year the population of Modakẹkẹ was estimated at 60,000.

Peace at Kiriji was made through the intercession of the Governor at Lagos. The armies were dispersed, and the walled war camps were burned to the ground. At that time it was estimated that there were 60,000 in the Ibadan camp and 40,000 in the camp of the Ekiti and their allies. However, no treaty was concluded with Ilọrin, and when the Ibadan troops withdrew, the Ilọrin army sacked Ọfa and butchered its inhabitants. The Ilọrin army continued to harass the Ibadan forces, which had withdrawn to Ikirun, until the latter returned to Ibadan in 1893 in accordance with treaties with the Governor of Lagos, which brought the Yoruba kingdoms in Nigeria under the Protectorate of Great Britain. Ilọrin continued to harass neighboring Yoruba towns until 1897, when it was occupied by forces of the Royal Niger Company.

The Postwar Period, 1893–1960

The century of warfare left profound effects on the Yoruba. Political boundaries were redrawn to conform to the *status quo* when peace was made, changing the size and shape of Yoruba kingdoms and placing the Yoruba in Ilọrin and Kabba Provinces in Northern Nigeria, while Ketu, Shabẹ, and other western groups came under French and German control. Ifẹ and Ilesha were placed in Ọyọ Province and Ibadan became an independent state, although it is still ruled by a town chief (Balẹ) rather than a king. The former kingdom of Owu was destroyed, many towns and villages were obliterated, and large areas were heavily depopulated. Refugees settled among different Yoruba subgroups, creating a degree of ethnic diversity, on a subgroup level, which had not existed previously, but which has increased steadily with the greater mobility that followed the establishment of the Pax Brittanica. The sixteen-year war left the Yoruba exhausted, anxious for peace, and willing to accept the British Protectorate, except for the Ilọrin, who were still trying to push the Jihad to the sea.

In 1894 the Ifẹ people returned home from Ishọya and Olubushe, also known as Adelẹkan, became Ọni and ruled until 1910. With peace established, European influences brought new changes to the old way of life, and the events which marked them have been remembered in later years as a means of reckoning time. In 1897 a narrow road was built near Ifẹ, and in 1900 the railway reached Ibadan. In 1901 Reverend Kayọde came to Ifẹ, and in 1903 Olubushe visited Lagos. In 1904 the first bicycle reached Ifẹ, causing a great commotion. In 1905 Olubushe built a two-story house inside the palace walls, with the first corrugated iron roof in town. In 1907 the first Nigerian penny reached Ifẹ. In 1909 Modakẹkẹ, which at the time was two or three times the size of Ifẹ, was finally dispersed, as had been called for in the peace treaty of 1886. Some of its inhabitants went to farms in the direction of Ibadan, and others went to live on their farms around Ifẹ.

Ajagun, who ruled as Ọni from June 1910 to June 1930, is also remembered as a tyrant, although he was described as a miserable weakling by Leo Frobenius when he visited Ifẹ in September 1910. When Frobenius saw him, Ajagun was dependent upon his chiefs because he was so new to office, but in later years he became independent and authoritarian. Frobenius' visit, which first brought the brass and terra-cotta heads of Ifẹ to the world's attention, is remembered as "the year the white man bought the gods of Ifẹ," referring to the collection of carvings and terra-cottas that he made. In 1912 the Native Administration Court was built, and in 1913 the Aiyetoro Church was built. In 1914 the first District Officer arrived, and in 1918 paper currency was introduced, due in part to a wartime shortage of metal for coins. In 1920 the Ọni's palace and its main gate were rebuilt, and the first automobile reached Ifẹ. In 1922 the people of Modakẹkẹ were given permission to resettle at their former site.

Atọbatẹlẹ (Sir Adesoji Aderẹmi) became Ọni in 1930. Following Nigeria's independence in 1960, he became the first Governor of the Western Region of Nigeria.

British Control, 1851–1960

The British, who had succeeded the Portuguese and the Dutch in the seventeenth century as masters of the slave trade to the Americas, had a change of heart and conscience, and in 1808 prohibited any slaves being carried on a British ship or landing in a British colony. Following this they assigned a naval squadron to patrol the Guinea Coast in an attempt to suppress the traffic in human beings. When this measure met with only limited success, they attempted to make treaties with African kings to suppress the slave trade. There can be no question of British sincerity in these attempts, but their treaties and actions clearly show that they also had a second motive, the development of British trade with West Africa.

Late in 1851 the British Consul entered the harbor of Lagos with ten ships of the naval squadron, with instructions to make a treaty for the abolition of the slave trade with the King of Lagos, as Lagos was a major slave port. With the Consul was Akitoye, who had been deposed as king by Kosoko, who then was King of Lagos. Following a fruitless conference with Kosoko, the Consul returned a second time and the ships were fired upon from the shore. On a third attempt, a rocket from the H.M.S. Bloodhound exploded a munitions magazine, starting a fire which destroyed most of Lagos, Kosoko escaped, but on January 1, 1852 the Consul signed a treaty with Akitoye, recognizing him as King of Lagos. Akitoye died three weeks later, and was succeeded by his son, Dosunmu.

In 1861, on the grounds that he had neither the power to suppress the slave trade nor to ensure good government, Dosunmu was summoned aboard the H.M.S. Prometheus and asked to sign a treaty ceding Lagos to the Queen of England, which he did on August 6, 1861. Later he protested that he had not understood the terms of the treaty which had, in any case, been forced upon him; thus the Colony of Lagos was established.

In 1884–1893 what is now known as the Eastern Region of Nigeria became a Protectorate of Britain, which was joined with the Western Region on January 1, 1900 to form the Southern Nigerian Protectorate. On the same date, the 1886 charter of the Royal Niger Company, which had established control over northern Nigeria, was cancelled and the Protectorate of Northern Nigeria was established. On January 1, 1914 the two protectorates and the colony were merged to form the Colony and Protectorate of Nigeria, and on October 1, 1960 Nigeria became an independent nation.

3

Economics

Subsistence Farming

THE YORUBA ECONOMY is based on sedentary hoe farming, craft specialization, and trade. Hunting, fishing, animal husbandry, and the gathering of wild foods are practiced, but the basis of the Yoruba diet consists of starchy tubers, grains, and plantains grown on their farms, supplemented by vegetable oils, wild and cultivated fruits and vegetables, and meat and fish. Yams are the staple food in Ife, but because of their expense and the prestige associated with serving them, they may be reserved for social occasions while in private the family relies on cassava, taro, maize, beans, or plantains. In Abeokuta Province some rice is grown, but cassava is the staple; and north of the rain forest, guinea corn (sorghum) and bulrush millet are important in the diet; but these four crops are not grown in significant quantities in Ife. Cocoa is the principal cash crop.

Chickens, guinea fowl, pigeons, ducks, and turkeys are kept as domestic fowl, and goats, sheep, pigs, dwarf cattle, horses, dogs, cats, rabbits, and guinea pigs as domestic animals. All of these, except cats, were eaten in former times. Wild birds and game are hunted in the forests and in the open grasslands, and fish and shrimp are caught in the larger rivers, the lagoon, and along the ocean. Professional hunters and fishermen sell their catch fresh through traders in the market or dry it for sale in areas where fish and game are less plentiful. With the increasing population and the expansion of cocoa-farming, large game has virtually disappeared in parts of the rain forest and hunters must be content with birds, snakes, snails, rats, and tortoises. During the twentieth century Zebu cattle, driven on foot from northern Nigeria, have been slaughtered and sold in the local markets.

In earlier days meat was a food for ceremonies and special occasions. Only the wealthy could afford to buy meat regularly in the market or to kill domestic animals simply for food. In common with many Africans elsewhere, many Yoruba ate meat only when an animal died or was sacrificed, and they might go for long periods without tasting meat. With the end of the wars of the nineteenth century, this situation has improved considerably; beef is usually available in the market and cocoa has provided more money to spend on food, but even in 1937 stews containing meat were still regarded as food of the well-to-do.

The predominance of starch in the diet is indicated by the fact that of fifty-six food recipes recorded in Ife, forty-seven consist of different ways of preparing yams, maize, plantains, cassava, and taro. Six are stews, which may or may not contain meat or fish; they are made of vegetable oil and are highly seasoned with salt and chile pepper. Of the remaining three, two are based on melon seeds and one is simply toasted peanuts.

Palm oil, extracted from the fibrous flesh outside the black shell of the nuts of the oil palm, has a reddish-orange color which is characteristic of many Yoruba dishes; it is not to be confused with the white palm kernel oil which is extracted from the kernel of the palm nut and used in making the black Yoruba soap. Palm oil is the most important of the vegetable oils used for food purposes; it is used in preparing stews and may be served with starchy dishes. Oil from melon seeds and locust beans are also used in Ife; peanut oil and shea butter are important farther north, and coconut oil nearer the coast. Women prepare palm oil, crack palm nuts to extract palm kernels, and shell melon seeds.

The oil palm is also a source of palm wine which is made by tapping the tree at the crown and collecting the sap in a gourd or bottle. Wine is also made from the bamboo or raffia palm, and beers are brewed from maize and guinea corn, and to a lesser extent from bananas and sugar cane. Kola nuts, which serve as a stimulant, are traditionally offered to guests and are an important export to the interior. Cotton, indigo, tobacco, and gourds or calabashes are also grown.

The farming cycle varies somewhat from region to region, but is regulated by the wet and dry seasons. In Ife the farmer cuts the bush to make a new farm plot in January or February, when there is little rain, lets it dry, and burns it. The second heavy task, hoeing yam heaps, follows in February or March. When the heaps of dirt have been prepared, sections from last year's yams are planted in them as seed. In the same period melons and the first crop of maize are planted, although some families rely on melon seeds imported from other towns. In April and May, sticks are cut and set out as tripods for the yam vines to grow on and, with the early rains, weeding of the fields begins. This is the lean period when there is little farm produce to eat.

By June or July the first crop of corn can be harvested, and by July or August new yams can be eaten. Three rituals mark the eating of new yams. Near the end of June the sixteen highest ranking priests of Ifa perform a new yam festival for the Oni and his palace retinue, and divine for them. In July they perform a similar ritual for themselves after which the worshipers of Ifa and the "white deities" can eat new yams. In August a new yam festival is performed by the worshipers of other deities, permitting them to eat new yams. Christians and Muslims may begin eating new yams in June or July.

In harvesting new yams, the crowns from which the vines sprout are cut off the larger roots and replanted in the heap where they continue to grow. This practice is continued until the final yam harvest in the dry season. In July or August the second crop of corn is planted, either between the rows of yam heaps or in a different field. In October beans are planted in the corn field or between the rows of yams. If corn and beans are grown in a yam field, they are planted between alternate rows of yam heaps. The final harvest of yams, corn, and beans comes in December and January, when the annual cycle begins again.

Yams and the second corn crop are planted on the plot in its second and third year, after which it is allowed to fallow for four or five years, when it must be cleared again before it is replanted. After this, two years of fallow between each three years of use are sufficient until the soil becomes "tired," and the plot is abandoned for ten or more years until it has reverted to bush and this cycle can be begun again. While one plot is fallow, a farmer uses other plots; and he plans a program which gives him plantable land each year. No fertilizers were used, except for leaves buried in yam heaps and wood ash, and irrigation was unnecessary, but the system of rotating the land by fallowing made possible a sedentary way of life and cities which have been in existence for centuries.

Farming is men's work, although a few women worked their farms like men. In Ondo women help their husbands more than in Ife, where men do the clearing, hoeing, planting, weeding, and harvesting. A wife may carry seed yams to the farm and lay them out on the yam heaps for her husband to plant; she may help him in harvesting corn, beans, or cotton; or she may carry his yams to market and sell them for him; but a man cannot ask his wife to hoe or clear a field; and if he even asks her to carry yam sticks to the farm he is called a tyrant.

A farmer usually works alone or with his unmarried sons; but several men who have farms near each other may agree to a labor exchange (aro), working together an equal number of days or hoeing the same number of heaps on the farm of each in turn. The host provides food, but this form of cooperative work does not require a large expenditure, and it can be used for planting and weeding as well as for clearing and hoeing one's own field. If a man misses a turn, he makes up the work he owes on another occasion.

Alternatively a man can invite his relatives, his friends, or the members of his club, depending on the size of the task, to form a working bee (owe). He provides food and drink for the group at the end of the day's work, but this is not considered payment; others participate because they earn the right to call upon their host for help under similar circumstances. No strict accounting is kept of an individual's participation; but if someone calls for working bees without taking part when others hold them, it is noticed and others will fail to respond to his invitation. Unlike some Yoruba towns, in Ife a man does not call for this type of cooperative work on his own farm, but only for the work required by his father-in-law, which may include clearing a field, hoeing yam heaps, or house building. Even in these cases working bees have been dying out in Ife as wage

(a) *The market at Meko, a town of about five thousand, 1950. Note the women's head ties.*

(b) *Tapping an oil palm for palm wine near Igana, 1938.*

(c) *Thatching a roof at Ife, 1938. Ife houses are thatched with broad leaves* (Sarcophrynium spp.) *rather than with grass, as at Oyo and Igana.*

Drumming at Ifẹ, 1937. The man at the right carries a pressure drum with brass bells around the drum head. The two instruments (shẹkẹrẹ) on the left are calabashes with cowry shells strung loosely on the outside. When twisted back and forth they serve as rattles; when the bottom is struck with the flat of the hand they serve as drums.

A woman's club singing and dancing in the streets of Ifẹ, 1937. The rhythm is beaten with the hands and folded, circular leather fans. Note the blouses of the same pattern, and the different hair styles.

laborers and money to hire them have become available; instead of joining the work group, men began to send money to hire laborers to take their places.

Until prohibited by law in the 1930s, wealthy farmers could have their farms worked by indentured laborers or "pawns" (iwọfa). A man who borrowed money for bridewealth or a funeral, for example, would agree to work for his creditor until the loan was repaid in full, his labor taking the place of interest. The arrangements varied and the amount of the loan and the work required were agreed upon through bargaining. A man might agree to plant and harvest 2000 yam heaps a year, to work on the creditor's farm a certain number of days each month, or to work for him in the morning while working his own land in the afternoon. In some cases a younger brother was indentured instead of the debtor, or a child was indentured to perform domestic work.

In still earlier times, when there were no wage laborers, the wealthy had Hausa and Nupe slaves to work their farms. These were purchased by traders in towns to the north and sold in Ifẹ. Yoruba from other towns were kidnapped when they were returning from the farm by Ifẹ raiding parties, but they were kept as house slaves and were treated much like a member of the family. Both farm and house slaves could own property and could buy their own freedom. Slavery ended in 1894, following the second return from Ishọya. As soon as the slaves learned that the British opposed slavery, many simply left their masters; those who felt themselves a part of the family remained, but they could no longer be considered or treated as slaves.

Cocoa: the Principal Cash Crop

Around 1900, cocoa was introduced to Ifẹ, and since about 1920 it has been the dominant factor in the economy, not only in Ifẹ, but throughout much of the forest belt. More than 99 percent of the total tonnage of Nigerian cocoa graded in 1940–1941 was produced in Yoruba territory, only 741 out of 97,862 tons coming from Benin and Warri provinces. Nigeria ranks third among the world's producers of cocoa, following Brazil and Ghana. By 1947 cocoa ranked first in terms of value among Nigeria's exports but since then, from year to year, it has fallen behind or been ahead of peanuts from the Northern Region. Since 1964, petroleum exports from the Eastern and Midwestern Regions have exceeded both these agricultural crops in terms of value. In Ifẹ new cocoa trees are planted in June or July and reach peak production in about eighteen years. They are weeded from May through July or August, and the main crop is harvested from September to December. The cocoa beans are fermented, graded for quality, and sold to trading firms for export. Women may help their husbands in harvesting and fermenting cocoa.

The introduction of cocoa has produced several changes at Ifẹ and other parts of the forest zone. Wage labor was attracted to the cocoa farms, replacing slaves and indentured laborers, and contributing to the decline of the working bee. A new source of credit became available as cocoa farmers could "pawn" their trees when they needed money; in this case the creditor could harvest them until the debt was repaid in full, the crops taking the place of interest. As more and more forest land has been cleared for cocoa trees, less has been available for food crops; yams and other foods have been imported in increasing quantities from towns north of the forests and, as already noted, large game has virtually disappeared. Because they have a long bearing life, the planting of cocoa trees in large numbers has also complicated the system of land tenure.

Land Tenure

Each clan owns its own farm land, granted originally by the king (Ọba) or the town chief (Balẹ). This is assigned to its members on the basis of individual need, and is subject to reassignment. Although a man's land may continue to be worked by his heirs, they own only the crops they grow on it. Trees like oil palms, kola trees, and cocoa are private property, owned by the person who plants them and later by his heirs. Thus one man may own a kola tree when another has the right to plant beneath it but no right to touch the kola nuts. With sections of land planted with groves of cocoa trees, beneath which other crops do not grow, the owner of the trees virtually becomes the owner of the land even though in theory it belongs to the clan as a whole. Outsiders are permitted to lease clan land for farming on condition that they pay an annual fee (ifọ, ishakọlẹ) as an acknowledgment of the clan's ownership; but when a tenant plants cocoa trees on the land, the clan may have to go to court to protect its right to it.

Craft Specialization and Trade

Nearly all Yoruba men engage in farming, but the production of many other goods is specialized. Weaving, dyeing, ironworking, brasscasting, woodcarving, calabash-carving, beadworking, leatherworking, and pottery, as well as hunting, fishing, drumming, divining, circumcising and cicatrizing, and the compounding of charms and medicines are crafts whose techniques are known only to a small group of professionals and are often protected as trade secrets by religious sanctions. Traders are also professionals, and in recent times sawyers, carpenters, brick makers, bricklayers, tailors, bicycle repairmen, automobile mechanics, shop keepers, letter writers and other professions have been added. Most of these specialists do some farming, but they supply all other members of the community with their goods and services.

Craft specialization makes each individual economically dependent upon the society as a whole. The carver depends upon the blacksmith for tools, and upon the farmer, the hunter, and the trader for food. The blacksmith depends upon others for food, and upon the weaver for clothing. The farmer depends on the smith for his hoe, machete, and axe, and on the weaver for his clothing. The weaver depends on the farmer for his food, and on the farmer, the spinner, and the dyer for his cotton thread. Each of these, moreover, must rely upon the herbalist, the priest, the potter, the drummer, the chief, and other specialists for goods and services which they can not provide for themselves.

Craft specialization also meant the development of internal trade and town markets for the exchange of local produce. The size and importance of these markets, visited by many tens of thousands in the larger cities, impress the visitor today as they did the early explorers. Bowen, an early American missionary who travelled through parts of Yoruba country in the 1850s, wrote:

> The most attractive object next to the curious old town itself—and it is always old —is the market. This is not a building, but a large area, shaded with trees, and surrounded and sometimes sprinkled over with little open sheds, consisting of a very low thatched roof surmounted on rude posts. Here the women sit and chat all day, from early morning till 9 o'clock at night, to sell their various merchandise. . . . The principal marketing hour, and the proper time to see all the wonders, is the evening. At half an hour before sunset, all sorts of people, men, women, girls, travelers lately arrived in the caravans, farmers from the fields, and artizans from their houses, are pouring in from all directions to buy and sell, and talk. At the distance of half a mile their united voices roar like the waves of the sea. . . . As the shades of evening deepen, if the weather allows the market to continue, and there is no moon, every woman lights her little lamp, and presently the market presents to the distant observer, the beautiful appearance of innumerable bright stars. . . . Every fifth day there is a "large market," when the few thousand people who attend daily are increased to a multitude (Bowen 1857:296–297).

In speaking of every fifth day, Bowen is following the custom of the Yoruba who, like the ancient Greeks, count both the first and last days. The Yoruba have thirteen lunar months composed of seven four-day weeks. Bowen is referring to the weekly markets which are held in rotation every four days; other markets, particularly in rural areas, are held every eight days or every sixteen days. The importance of markets in Yoruba life is suggested by the fact that in Ifẹ the days of the week are named for the markets held on them: Ọja Ifẹ, the market of Ifẹ in front of the Ọni's palace, Ita Irẹmọ in Irẹmọ ward; Aiyegbaju in Aiyegbaju precinct in Ilode ward; and Ita Ikọgun in Ikọgun ward. Days are named after markets in other Yoruba towns as well, or after deities (Ifa, Ogun, Shango, and Orishala).

The markets are composed of areas occupied by women selling the same commodities: poultry in basketry coops, tethered goats and sheep, yams, peppers, plantains, green vegetables, meat, salt, palm oil, palm wine, soap, cloth, pots, firewood, the varied ingredients of charms and medicines, and European cloths and other imported items. They are dominated by women traders, the principal exception being the men who butcher and sell cattle from the north. During the day, before the market reaches its peak, women hawk their wares through town or sell them in front of the house and at street corners. Many women prepare and sell cooked food in the streets or scattered through the market. Over a century ago Bowen (1857:301) observed, "No people are so much in the habit of eating in the streets, where women are always engaged in preparing all sorts of dishes for sale to passers by."

A farmer's wife may carry his produce to market and sell it for him, turning over the full sale price to her husband; but many women are professional traders.

Some pay cash for their goods and others take their goods on credit; both trade for profit, bargaining with both the producer and the consumer in order to obtain as large a margin of profit as possible. Bargaining is a standard feature of Yoruba economic transactions. Other women traders are commissioned agents who deal regularly with a particular producer; a weaver, for example, may show his agent cloths that he wishes to be sold and tell her the price he expects to receive for them. If she believes that the price is right, she takes them on credit; when they have been sold she pays the weaver what he asked and in return she receives a commission, usually about five percent. If she cannot sell the cloths at the weaver's price, she can return them to him; but if she can sell them at higher prices, she earns a profit in addition to her commission.

A fourth system is followed by the women who sell palm wine, which cannot be sold when it is two days old, and brings only half price when it is a day old. Each palm wine tapper has a group of women who sell for him, each receiving the same amount each day to sell at the price set by the tapper. All the money received on the first two days belongs to the tapper, and that received on the third day belongs to his agent. If she should drop her calabash on the way to market, she or the tapper takes the loss depending upon whose day it is. A tapper is not concerned about how well an agent does on her own day, but he demands that she be reasonably successful in selling on his days, and if she is not he refuses to deal with her again.

The Guild of Importers

Women traders deal largely in local produce. Some have been able to obtain credit running into thousands of pounds sterling for imported goods, which they retail through their associates. In the last century, however, they could obtain merchandise produced outside of Ife only from a guild of importers known as Ipanpa, which is said to have had two hundred members, most of whom were men. All European trade goods, merchandise from other towns, and slaves passed through the hands of the Ipanpa, who resold them in town to women traders or directly to the consumers. Members of the Ipanpa went south to Ijebu towns, the main source of European goods, travelling in armed bands because of the dangers of war and the possibility of being enslaved themselves. They could sell the goods they brought back, but they had to give half their profit to Pakoyi, the head of the guild.

When traders came from Ijebu, Lagos, or other towns, they were not permitted to retail their goods in Ife. They sought out the Ipanpa representative in charge of the ward in which they had found lodging, and were taken to the Pakoyi. The Pakoyi bargained for the whole or a part of their merchandise, and, if no agreement was reached, they had to take their goods to another town. Whatever the Pakoyi purchased he distributed to the Ipanpa members who resold it in Ife. Again half of the daily profits was turned over to the Pakoyi the following morning, when the Ipanpa met at his house and ate together. The title Pakoyi or Parakoyi is also recognized at Ijebu Ode, Abeokuta, Ibadan, and Oyo.

One of the clauses of the 1893 treaties establishing the British Protectorate was a pledge by the kings "to use every means in our power to foster and promote trade." The monopoly of the Ipanpa was broken about 1911 or 1912 when European trading firms obtained permission from the Ǫni and his chiefs to establish stores selling directly to consumers, following which the guild disintegrated. At about the same time, toll gates were abolished.

Money and Credit

Although tradition speaks of a time when goods were bartered, money in the form of cowry shells was the basis of trade for many centuries, and tradition also tells of cowries being found in the lagoon. As M. D. W. Jeffreys has shown, cowry shells were in circulation in Ghana and in the Songhay and Melle kingdoms before the arrival of the Portuguese,[1] who soon began importing them.

In 1515 the King of Portugal issued a license to import cowry shells from India to Sao Tome; by 1522 they were being imported into Nigeria from the Malabar Coast, and during the seventeenth century from the East Indies. This resulted in their steady depreciation. In the middle of the nineteenth century the value of 2000 cowries was four shillings six pence, but it soon fell to less than two shillings when cheaper cowries were imported from Zanzibar. When cowries were replaced by coins, the value of 2000 cowries was stabilized at six pence for ritual purposes, or 80,000 to the pound sterling. Cowries were counted in strings of 40, in bunches of 200 (5 strings), in "heads" of 2000 (10 bunches), and in bags of 20,000 (10 heads) weighing 60 pounds.

Credit was available from money lenders at high rates of interest, through the institution of indenture or "pawning" and, since the introduction of cocoa, through the "pawning" of cocoa trees. It also was and is available through the esusu, an institution which has elements similar to installment buying, a credit union, and a savings club. The esusu is a fund to which a group of individuals make fixed contributions of money at fixed intervals; and the total amount contributed each period is assigned to each of the members in rotation. The number of contributors, the size of the contributions, and the length of the interval between contributions vary from one group to another; but if twenty members contribute one shilling each monthly, at the end of twenty months, which completes the cycle, each member will have contributed one pound and will have received one pound in return. There is neither gain nor loss; but the advantage to the members is that they have one pound in a lump sum (or larger amounts of money if there are more members or larger contributions) with which to purchase goods, pay for services, or repay debts. Except for the one who receives the fund at the end of a cycle, all members receive an advance on their contributions without having to pay interest. Moreover, an attempt is made to make the fund available to members at times when they have need for it, assigning it to a member who applies for it unless he has been tardy in making his payments or has already received the fund during the current cycle.

---

[1] *American Anthropologist*, Vol. 50, 1948: 46-47.

As noted initially, the foundations of the economy in precontact times were sedentary hoe farming, craft specialization, and farming. The rotation of crops and, particularly, the rotation of land through fallowing made possible a sedentary way of life and the development of large, dense, permanent communities and an urban way of life. Craft specialization led to trade, both within and between these communities, and made each individual economically dependent upon the society as a whole. Trade involved professional middlemen, formal markets, and money. The pecuniary nature of Yoruba culture and the importance of the profit motive are both apparent.

4

Government

The Kingdom

A S WE HAVE SEEN, the authority of the Yoruba kings is validated by the myth of the creation of the earth by Odua and of the subsequent dispersion of his sixteen sons to found the original Yoruba kingdoms. Regardless of its fanciful elements, this myth is still a vital element in local politics. The Yoruba continue to debate whether or not one or another of the hundred kings who today wear beaded crowns are the direct descendants of Odua's sons. In the large three-volume report of the Martindale Commission which was held in 1937 to determine the right of the Akarigbo of Ijebu Remo to wear a beaded crown, it was found that he was directly descended from Odua and had migrated from Ife as a crowned king, a finding with which many Yoruba disagreed.

Despite this claim of a common origin, there is marked variation in the political structures of the Yoruba kingdoms. Peter Lloyd (1965:551) is probably right when he says "One could, I think, write a textbook on comparative political systems, drawing almost all one's examples from the Yoruba!" Rather than attempting a general survey, this case study will be restricted to the political structure of the kingdom of Ife, where it is believed that the earth was created.

Ife, or more properly Ile-Ife, is the capital of a kingdom of moderate size, about 70 miles long and 40 miles wide, before the wars of the nineteenth century.[5] As its king, the Oni ruled over the capital through his town chiefs (Ife), and over the outlying towns through the Ife town and palace chiefs, the five provincial chiefs, and the local town chiefs (Bale). Obalaye at Alaye, about 7 miles from Ife, controlled some ninety towns in the direction of Ijebu in the southwest; but these were destroyed and abandoned just prior to the Owu war. Obawara at Iwara ruled to the Oni River in the direction of Ondo in the southeast; only Ifetedo remains of the former towns in this division. Onpetu at Ido, about 2 miles from Ife, ruled

---

[5] On the frontispiece map, the old northern boundary of the kingdom is shown as —|—|
—|—.

29

some seventy towns in the direction of Ilesha toward the northeast; but the six surviving towns in this division (including Oshu and Iloba) are under Ilesha today. Owafegun at Oke Awo ruled to Ejigbo in the direction of Old Oyo toward the northwest, and Obalejugbe at Ijugbe ruled to Ikire and the Oshun River in the direction of Ibadan toward the west; but most of the towns in these two provinces are now under Ibadan.

These provincial chiefs collected tribute from the town chiefs within their jurisdiction and divided it with the Oni; they and their town chiefs were subject to the Oni, but they had jurisdiction over internal affairs as long as they remained loyal and things went smoothly. During the wars of the last century they and their surviving followers moved to Ife, and Obalaye gave up his palace and beaded crown. As the highest ranking provincial chief, Obalaye was made representative of the foreigners living in Ife. He claims descent from an early Oni, but explains that his ancestor was exiled from the palace because he was born within its walls; it is an evil sign for anyone to be born or die in the Oni's palace. It is said that if three Oni died during the office of an Obalaye, he was chosen to succeed them.

Ife itself is divided into five wards (adugbo), each comprising a number of precincts (ogbon), headed by ward chiefs and precinct chiefs. Each precinct is made up of a number of compounds headed by the eldest male clan member. The compounds are large, complex, rectangular structures, housing up to several hundred inhabitants, with rooms arranged around one or more open patios. Formerly they had windowless mud walls and gabled roofs thatched with broad leaves; newer houses have wooden shutters or glass windows, cement or brick walls, sheet metal roofs, and are two or three stories high, in an architectural style introduced by freed slaves who returned from Brazil. Since 1937–1938 many of these new houses have been built in parts of Ife which had been unoccupied since the wars of the last century.

The King

Yoruba kings are distinguished by the right to wear beaded crowns, the symbols of their authority. Some of these are made of imported glass beads with sixteen three-dimensional beaded birds attached to them; others are made of red stone beads. A new state crown is made at the installation of each Oni, but some beads from the crown of his predecessor are used to preserve the link to Odua. Beaded caps may be worn in place of the state crown so that the king's head may not be uncovered. In addition some kings, including the Oni, have beaded gowns and sandals and large beaded parasols, cushions, ram's beard whisks, and staffs. The right to use solidly beaded materials is a prerogative reserved to royalty and to the Ifa diviners, but the diviners are not permitted to wear beaded crowns. State crowns, except for that of the Owa of Ilesha, have bead fringes which cover the king's face, which was formerly not to be seen by his associates. In earlier times no one could eat with the king, nor could he be seen eating or drinking.

In many respects Yoruba kings are divine. It is said that in the remote past the Oni were sacrificed to Odua after ruling only one or two years, but there is no way of knowing the truth of this legend; since 1849 there have been only five Ọni and one interregnum. However, even though they are considered direct descendants of Odua, they could be deposed for strictly political reasons. When their rule was unpopular, mobs of people demonstrated outside the palace walls, the chiefs met at the palace gate, sent word to the king that he was no longer wanted, and then refused to answer his call. When this happened, informants say, he opened a "calabash of death" containing a powerful charm made of parrots' eggs which was kept for such an occasion, and the sight of it killed him. It was no more possible for him to escape in former times than it was for slaves to run away from their masters; but if he took refuge with Araba, the head of the diviners, he was permitted to live in exile. If an Ọni refused to commit suicide in this way, the Oro cult joined the crowds at night with bullroarers whirling, and he was killed by Oro. The Egungun cult joined the crowds also, but kept apart from Oro. According to tradition an Ọni named Akinmọyero (also known as Ọdunlẹ, the fourth Ọni before Abeweila) was dragged from his palace by the Oro and beheaded because he was selling Ifẹ people into slavery, permitting them to be captured by Ọyọ refugees living in outlying towns in the kingdom.

The king's person was sacred and he was isolated in his palace (afin) from the people he ruled. Following the crowning of a new Ọni of Ifẹ, he moved into the palace, and he could return home to visit his relatives only incognito and under the cover of darkness. He appeared in public only once a year, at the major sacrifice to Ogun, the God of Iron, and even then he was concealed behind cloths held by his messengers so that only his crown and its white egret feather could be seen. During the festival of Orishala he made three trips from the palace to the shrine, but on these occasions all the townspeople of Ifẹ had to remain in their houses with their windows closed and the women worshipers waiting at the shrine had to lie down with cloths over their heads so that he would not be seen.

The journey of the Ọni to Lagos in 1903 was a historic event because it was the first of its kind; there was much weeping in Ifẹ at his departure, and the other Yoruba kings lived outside their palaces until he returned. It was not until 1925, on the occasion of the visit of the Prince of Wales, that the Yoruba kings first met face to face at Ibadan. In 1904 and again in 1937 the Alake of Abẹokuta visited England, following which several Yoruba kings made visits abroad; partly as the result of these travels, the seclusion of the kings has been ended. By 1937 the Oni appeared in public almost daily without having his face covered, driving openly through the streets in his Buick touring car.

The Ọni is chosen from the royal patrilineal clan; this is the largest clan in Ifẹ with over twenty compounds and more than five thousand members in 1937. His position is hereditary, but like many other titles of priests and chiefs which are "owned" by particular clans, it does not pass from father to son. Males of four lineages or branches of the royal clan are eligible to become king in rotation, but lineages are skipped if they have no suitable candidates, and the same lineage may even provide two Ọni in succession. Each of the eligible compounds may campaign for its own candidate by spending money in entertaining the town and palace chiefs, who select the king, and by deferring to all who may influence them in their final choice. While one of their number rules as Ọni, the other members of

his compound can count on his protection and can take advantage of the townspeople; but the members of the other royal compounds rank beneath the townspeople because they must be careful of their behavior lest they gain a reputation
for arrogance or selfishness which would decrease the chances of their future
candidates.

Wealth is important in these campaigns but it is not an essential qualification for a king or a chief; nor is a candidate selected simply on the basis of how
much he and his family spend, although this is a measure of his generosity and
of how well he is liked by those who know him best. The main objective is to
select the best candidate; and the qualities which are most important are good
character, unselfishness, and willingness to listen to advice. Sex is also an important
qualification for political office, but according to Ifẹ traditions, women ruled as
Ọni at least twice in the remote past. Seniority is not a factor, although it may
have been in earlier times. The candidate must be at least about thirty years of age,
he should be married, and his father must be dead; no chief should have a father
to whom he must bow. In recent years older candidates have been rejected in order
to have someone who has been to school, who is literate in both English and
Yoruba, and who has had experience in dealing with Europeans, Sir Adesoji
Aderẹmi had been an employee of the Nigerian Railway before he became Ọni
in 1930. Competing for title also may be more common than in the past, when a
person might simply be notified that he had been selected for office.

According to an Ifẹ legend, at the death of one Ọni the king's messengers
went to Adagba, a wealthy man who was eligible to succeed, and told him that the
Ọni was hungry and wanted money from him. He replied sarcastically, "*He* wants
me to send him money? Does he keep his money in *my* pocket? Where he sits
in the palace, can *he* go hungry?" The messengers then went to Otutu, his younger
brother who was at his farm, and delivered the same message. Otutu prostrated
himself, saying, "My father remembers me here in the farm. While I am alive,
he will not starve." Otutu gave the messengers food and drink and sent them back
with twenty slaves carrying goats, chickens, and farm produce. The next day the
death of the Ọni was announced and Otutu returned home. Adagba was certain he
would be chosen to succeed because of his wealth, and on the day set for the
selection of the new Ọni he had food prepared, dressed himself in the fine clothes
he had provided for the occasion, and sat down to await the messengers who would
inform him. They passed him by and took Otutu, having to use force because he
had not expected to be chosen. Since that time no one in Adagba compound can
be made Ọni, even though they are patrilineal descendants of the royal clan. This
legend sets a respected precedent for choosing the most loyal and generous candidate
for office, but there is a question as to whether such candidates are still so often
chosen today when other qualifications for office are becoming more seriously
considered.

Wanikin compound is related to the royal clan through a female and, while
its members are considered to belong to it, they are not eligible to become Ọni.
Instead this compound owns the title of Shoko Wanikin, the official head of the
royal clan, with a series of subordinate Shoko titles which are filled from other
royal compounds. The Shoko are responsible for the affairs of the royal clan, and

they meet every sixteen days to eat and drink and discuss matters affecting the clan. The third step in becoming Ọni is to take a Shoko title temporarily.

A new Ọni is responsible for the wives of his predecessors as well as his own, and they continue to live in their quarters in the palace. In 1938, the total number of king's wives was estimated to be about one hundred. They are known as chiefs or "Heads" (Olori) and are under the "Mother of the Heads" (Yeye Olori), the one who has been the wife of a king for the longest time. If any of her co-wives were disrespectful to the "Mother," she could be stripped naked and whipped. Until about 1930, when the custom was changed, the Ọni took the widows of his predecessors as his own wives. Formerly their hair was shaved so as to leave a short oval tuft of hair in the center of the head, but now they wear their hair like other women.

The Town Chiefs and Palace Chiefs

The town chiefs (Ifẹ) are Ọruntọ, head of Irẹmọ ward, Ejio of Mọrẹ ward, Ọbalọran of Ilode ward, Jagunoshin, Washin of Ilare ward, Ejesi, Akọgun of Ikọgun ward, and Ọbalaye who represents the foreigners who have settled in Ifẹ. There is a saying, "Six Ifẹ, a foreigner makes the seventh," referring to Ọbalaye but omitting Akọgun, an important war chief, who like Ọbalaye was formerly just an observer. Beneath each of the five ward chiefs are five other chiefs known by the same title (Balẹ) as the chiefs of the outlying towns; they are appointed by the ward chiefs and are responsible for the young adults in their wards. Modakẹkẹ is now recognized as a sixth ward, under its Balẹ, but it is represented in Ifẹ government only through Ọbalaye. The five ward chiefs and Ọbalaye are each chosen from a particular clan, and their titles are clan property. Jagunoshin and Ejesi may be chosen from any Ifẹ ward and are subordinate to its chief. There are other lesser Ifẹ chiefs,[6] but these eight are responsible to the Ọni for the administration of the capital, and they represent the interests of the townspeople at the palace.

Ọruntọ is also known as "King of the town of Ifẹ" (Ọbalufẹ, Ọba ilu Ifẹ) and as "Ọni of the outside" (Ọni ode) because he rules outside the palace, in contrast to the king himself who is "Ọni of the house" (Ọni ile). Ọbalọran's compound provided a refuge for anyone who had offended the Ọni or committed a crime, including murder; if Ọbalọran asked that he be set free, the request could not be refused. If a prisoner was taken past Ọbalọran's house he could cry "Ọbalọran help me" and he had to be released to him; usually prisoners were taken by other routes to avoid this, but anyone who cried "I grasp the post of Ọbalọran" while he was being arrested, was released to Ọbalọran's custody.

The head of the elder women of Ifẹ held the title "Mother Ojumu" (Yeye Ojumu) whose relationship to them resembled that of Ọruntọ to the men of Ifẹ. She was assisted by the "Mother at the market" (Yeyeloja, Yeye li ọja) who was

---

[6] Three of these were war chiefs, Lodi, Shigbunshin, and Lukosi; like Jagunoshin, Washin, and Ejesi, they were formerly assistants to Ọruntọ, Ejio, and Ọbalọran respectively.

in charge of the market women and settled disputes between them. The title of "Mother at the outside" (Iyalode) which is used in Oyo and elsewhere for the head of the townswomen was introduced only recently into Ife, and is not important.

In addition there are eight important palace chiefs (Woye); Lowa Ijaruwa, Jaran, Aguro, Arode, Shanire, Ladin, Lowate, and Erebese, followed by minor palace chiefs and the king's messengers or pages. They are assigned to three ritual chambers in the palace, with Lowa, Arode, and Lowate in charge of Ile Ogungun and its deity, Odua; Jaran, Shanire, and Erebese in charge of Ile Ominrin and the deity Orishala; and Aguro and Ladin responsible for Ile Iloshin and Oramfe, the Ife God of Thunder who was sent to earth to keep peace between Odua and Orishala. In addition to their other functions, the palace chiefs and the king's messengers were responsible for religious rituals performed within the palace and for representing the Oni at the many religious festivals held at the shrines in town. Although perhaps less important than the adjudication of disputes, this was a major task because there were only twenty-five days during the year when no festivals were being performed.

The palace chiefs have the responsibility of representing the interests of the Oni in dealing with the Ife town chiefs and with outlying towns within the kingdom. The chiefs of Ile Ogungun were the intermediaries between the Oni and the town of Moro, and received tribute from it for the Oni. Those of Ile Ominrin served in the same fashion for the town of Ashipa and for the blacksmiths and hunters, as did those of Ile Iloshin for the town of Ipetumodu and the woodcarvers. The Ife town chiefs also served as intermediaries for outlying towns, with Obaloran receiving tribute to the Oni from Edunabon and Iwo.

The palace chiefs are chosen from individuals with the status of Modewa, which is distinct from that of the royal clan, the Ife clans, and the strangers from other towns. The reason for this distinction is not clear, but it is usually explained that in return for assistance to an Oni in the remote past, he permitted the ancestors of the three Modewa clans to live inside the palace gate (Enuwa Geru) where their compounds were located, until the palace walls were shortened, leaving them outside. They did not belong to any of the five quarters, but were directly under the Oni, and they were called servants or "boys of the king" (omode owa) which was contracted to Modewa. In time these compounds became so crowded that their clans were forced to found new compounds in various parts of town; there is an Ife saying that "If a house is squeezed at Enuwa, they separate and go to Ode Egbudu precinct" (Ile lo fun l'Enuwa, won r'Ode Egbudu). Those who left the palace lost their status as Modewa and became Ife, as in the case of Ile Lukosi Odo, Ile Adaja, and Ile Oshogun; as another saying goes, "If we should move to town, we join them" (Ilu a ba ya re, l'a ba pe).

Thus this status is not strictly hereditary. An Ife man may become a Modewa, and his children after him, if he is wealthy enough to afford two expensive initiations (arapon, idoko) so as to become a man of leisure (Lodoko) and spend his days in the palace. This is a step toward taking a title, and it frees a man from serving on labor levies, being sent on errands, and having property expropriated; they pay taxes today, but formerly they were exempt from paying tribute. If a Modewa becomes an Ife town chief, for example,

Jagunoshin or Ejesi, he becomes an Ifẹ but his relatives prefer to remain Mọdewa. It is said that there are more Mọdewa than Ifẹ today.

Although the palace chiefs are spoken of as servants of the king, and although they rank somewhat below the Ifẹ town chiefs, there are advantages to being a Mọdewa, because they have access to the palace and to the king, whereas, unless they are summoned, the town chiefs came to the palace only every fourth day when they sat outside the gate to hear disputes. This continued until the Native Court system was instituted by the British, after which the town and palace chiefs both came into the palace to report to the Ọni on the cases they had heard. Before this the palace chiefs (Woye) and the king's messengers (Ẹmẹsẹ) served as the intermediaries between the Ifẹ town chiefs and the Ọni, reporting on cases heard and favors requested of them. Because of his isolation the Ọni had no way of checking on what actually had been said, and it was possible for the palace chiefs to alter the messages somewhat to their own advantage. The Mọdewa also were generally in a position to learn from the palace chiefs and the king's messengers what was going on in the palace and in town in a way that the town chiefs and the other people of Ifẹ did not. Even today they know the Ọni's plans before the Ifẹ do.

The Ẹmẹsẹ, Ogungbẹ, and Ogboni

When a palace chief dies, his eldest son is taken to join the Ogungbẹ or police, the second to become an Ẹmẹsẹ or page of the king, and the youngest to join the Ogboni which functioned as a senior law court. When a town chief dies, his sons are taken for the Ogungbẹ and the Ogboni, but not for the Ẹmẹsẹ. If there are no sons, younger brothers or brother's sons may be substituted. If the chief himself has not joined the Ogboni, his son does not do so.

The Ẹmẹsẹ, numbering over one hundred, are palace retainers who rank below the palace chiefs and run errands and carry messages for them and for the Ọni. They stay in the palace on a verandah (oke Ẹmẹsẹ) set aside for them, awaiting their assignments. They are appointed to the three chambers in the palace under the palace chiefs, a boy joining the group to which his father belonged. The Ẹmẹsẹ assist the palace chiefs in performing the religious rituals for which they are responsible. In earlier times the palace chiefs were chosen from among the Ẹmẹsẹ, because they were familiar with the palace routine from many years of experience; in recent times it has become increasingly common for other Mọdewa to compete for these titles and the rituals have suffered accordingly. Sons of the king's diviners (Awo Ọni), of the Ẹmẹsẹ, and of men of leisure (Lodọkọ) are also eligible to become Ẹmẹsẹ. The Ẹmẹsẹ are headed by Yegbata, who assigns their duties as Logun does within the compound (See Chapter 5). They are readily recognizable as representatives of the king because the right and left halves of their heads are shaved alternately every four days. When the Ọni makes his public appearance at the sacrifice for Ogun, they wear lumps of mud on their head, symbolizing the God of Medicine.

The Ẹmẹsẹ of Ile Ominrin were responsible for bringing couples charged with incest to trial. If found guilty they had to provide a he-goat which was killed for Ọrẹ, a Hunter God, and each was given a foreleg of the animal with which to beat each other. As they did so the woman asked "Why did you make love to me?" and the man responded "When I made love to you, why did you not refuse?"

The Ogungbẹ were the Ọni's bodyguard and the town police. They were divided into two sections, one composed of Mọdewa headed by Egbedi, and the other composed of townspeople under Ọlọmọde Ifẹ, the public executioner. Each had its own underground dungeon (gbere) where criminals were kept while awaiting trial; prisoners were kept there no more than six months until they were executed or released. For minor offenses the Ẹmẹsẹ were sent to summon people to court, but if an insane person (were) ran amuck or if a burglar, murderer, or traitor was at large, the Ogungbẹ were sent to apprehend them and hold them in the dungeon until they were executed at a place called Mesi Alukunrin. If the death penalty were commuted, the Ogungbẹ received a share of the money that the family paid. The Ogungbẹ were also responsible for securing the victims when human sacrifices were required. These were not common in Ifẹ, but the Ọni was formerly expected to provide a man at the annual festival at Odua and a woman at the annual festival of Orishala, and a man at his crowning when he built the mud dais which served as his throne. For many years now goats of the appropriate sex have been substituted on these occasions, but formerly a condemned criminal was sacrificed. If there was no one in the dungeon, the Ogungbẹ went out at night and seized any solitary person they came upon in the streets; a person seized could secure his release if a slave was provided to be sacrificed in his place.

Similarly the Ogungbẹ or the Ẹmẹsẹ secured the goats and sheep for the many sacrifices for which the Ọni was responsible, seizing animals that were wandering loose in the streets. During the day, the Ogungbẹ and the Ogboni sat with the Ẹmẹsẹ in the palace, but neither had to be present as the Ẹmẹsẹ did and neither could enter the Ẹmẹsẹ's ritual chambers. The police functions of the Ogungbẹ ended with the establishment of the Native Administration police, but they still secure sacrificial animals and participate in the ceremonies of installation of the town chiefs.

The Ogboni meet every sixteen days in their special house (Ile Mọlẹ) in Irẹmọ ward where they eat, dance, and perform rituals in the worship of the Earth. When a chief dies his family provides a ram, fifty kola nuts, twelve bottles of schnapps, and lots of food for a feast for the Ogboni, at the cost of $35.00 in 1937. This permits his successor to enter the Ogboni house as a "child of secret" (ọmọ awo), but he can only "crawl" as he danced until he pays the extra costs of becoming a man of leisure. Anyone who becomes a town or palace chief is expected to join the Ogboni a month after his installation but this can be postponed because of the lack of money. In 1937 there were about one hundred Ogboni members, all male.

The ritual symbols of the Ogboni are pairs of short staves (ẹdan Ogboni) cast in brass in human form and joined by brass chains. If anyone in town has difficulty in collecting a debt, he may come to Apena, the Ogboni chief, for assistance. Apena sends his symbols to the house of the debtor and they are laid on the verandah. No one may enter the verandah until the symbols are removed, and the debt must be repaid that day because the symbols must not remain there overnight. If the debtor is not home, other members of the family must pay what is owed. Both the debtor and the creditor pay a fee to Apena for this.

If human blood is shed on the ground in a fight, it is reported to Apena who sends his messengers to lay his Ogboni symbols beside the spot. Because of the power of the Earth God, who has been profaned by the blood, the parties to the fight must return and surrender themselves to the messengers who take them to the Ogboni house where they are tried. When their accounts cannot be reconciled and it is apparent that one party is lying, both are required to take an oath on the Earth known as "drinking ground" (imule, imu-ile), in the belief that if they swear falsely they will die.

The Ogboni constituted the second highest tribunal in Ife. If the chiefs could not settle a dispute it was referred to the Ogboni house where it was heard by the members who were concealed behind palm fronds. Because the plaintiff and defendant could not see them and did not know which members were for or against them, the Ogboni court was the most respected and feared as well as the most impartial. The legal functions of the Ogboni also disappeared with the establishment of the Native Administration Court. Initially this court was adjourned in difficult cases so that they could be discussed in the privacy of the Ogboni house; but this practice was discontinued because decisions were subject to review in the higher courts, eroding the authority of the judges and diminishing the importance of their decisions. Today the functions of the Ogboni are essentially ritual and social.

The Ogungbe, the Emese, and the Oni's wives could take their food from the market women, a little from each trader, without payment, and they could share in the food collected at the toll gates. There were eight gates in the town walls which were locked each night, at each of which a gate keeper (onibode) was formerly stationed. He took a small portion of each person's burden of yams, corn, or plantain from those returning from farms, and he shared it with the Ogungbe and the people of the palace. Those bringing palm oil from the farm tied a small calabash of oil to the side of their large calabash, and emptied it into a pot at the toll gate; each season eight huge pots were filled and given to the king. Traders coming to town had to pay a toll in cowry shells. In earlier days the toll gates were kept by slaves who lived in houses near them; but from about 1896 to about 1911, when they were abolished, they were kept by Emese.

The king also received gifts from his subjects, including slaves who worked his farms; he shared in fines, court fees, and the expenditures made by people when they took titles; and he received half of the fees collected by the five provincial chiefs for the use of their lands. Each provincial chief also brought one dog, ten snails, and ten tortoises annually; hunters, blacksmiths, and woodcarvers brought annual gifts of meat, knives, and wooden bowls. Under the 1893 treaty establishing the British Protectorate, annual salaries for the kings were substituted for the various forms of tribute, but many gifts have continued, probably on a reduced scale. In 1937 the blacksmiths brought the Oni twenty-five knives, each worth a penny and a half. For his part, the king was responsible for sacrifices and medicines for the good of his subjects, for entertaining those who brought gifts and other guests with food and drink, and for maintaining his palace and its retinue on an economic level appropriate to his position.

Other Officials

Several other groups are associated with government. Sixteen Otu priests dispose of sacrifices made in the palace, make atonements, and are in charge of the installation of the Ọni, the principal chiefs, and the priest of Odua. In earlier times, whenever the Ọni sent messengers to other towns, they were accompanied by members of the guild of traders and Pakoyi, its head, settled disputes concerning trading. The Ijẹgbẹ collected tribute from the townspeople of Ifẹ for Lọwa Ijaruwa, the top ranking palace chief, who served as treasurer; they were organized into separate groups under the head man of leisure (Olori Lodọkọ) of each of the five wards, of the Mọdewa, and of the strangers from other towns. The Isọgan, also organized in terms of wards, supervised the able bodied men when they were called upon to form working bees to thatch the palace, repair its walls, weed its grounds, or do other public works.

The war chiefs, headed by Balogun, led the men who volunteered in time of war, each joining the ranks of the chiefs in charge of his ward or the ranks of one of the subsidiary war chiefs holding Ifẹ titles. Neither group of war chiefs had civil authority in times of peace, although Akọgun was their representative among the Ifẹ town chiefs. The war chiefs became wealthy men because they received half of the slaves captured by their followers; they provided the guns and ammunition, and each soldier was responsible for his own food. The Ọni and the town and palace chiefs, except for Akọgun and the other war chiefs, remained at home in time of war to rule the kingdom. The war chief titles are now simply honorific, and the functions of these other groups have become less important due to the influence of Christianity and Islam, the imposition of taxes, and the use of corrugated iron sheets and cement for the palace roofs and walls.

The Legal System

In former times disputes which could not be settled within the clan and those involving different clans were referred to the ward chief. If members of different wards were involved or if the judgement of the ward chief was not accept-able to one of the parties, the case could be referred to the palace chiefs who met daily outside the palace gate and jointly with the town chiefs every fourth day (ojọ Ọja Ifẹ). If the matter were serious and involved members of Ifẹ clans, the town chiefs were summoned regardless of what day it was. Their decision was referred to the Ọni for his approval and if no decision could be reached, the case was referred to the Ogboni house. Beyond this, the last court of appeal, which rarely met, was held at the palace and included the town and palace chiefs, other Ogboni members, and the Ọni himself. In the outlying towns within the kingdom, cases were heard by the court of the town chief (Balẹ), but judgements calling for capital punishments were referred to Ifẹ. The right to execute criminals was formerly a prerogative which distinguished Yoruba kings (Ọba) from uncrowned town chiefs (Balẹ) and, except for the Ọwa of Ilesha who was given a sword by Odua, the Alafin of Ọyọ and the other Yoruba kings received their state sword from Ifẹ when they were crowned.

Aside from this series of courts, disputes can be adjudicated informally. On one occasion a fight broke out in the street between a tailor and a woman who owed him three pence. As she had been passing his shop, the tailor asked her for his money, and one of his apprentices grabbed her by her skirt. The other apprentices began clapping at her and crying in rhythm, "Hey, hey, hey, hey." At this she became angry and demanded of the tailor, "What have I done to be clapped at in this way? Is a debt of three pence cause enough for me to be treated so? What have I done to deserve this?" As the tailor had no answer, she began striking, rather ineffectually, at him. At this point an elderly man got between them, taking a stick to separate them but not striking anyone with it. As he was anxious to have the dispute settled so that he could leave, he called to the acting head of the nearest compound to stop them.

When the compound head told them to stop, they did so even though the woman was still tense with anger. If they had continued to fight, the one who struck the first blow after having been told to stop would have been judged guilty. The woman was asked to speak, then the tailor, then the woman, and then the man again. If either had interrupted the other, he or she would have been told to keep quiet and would have been shoved and hit until he did so. As it turned out, the woman had gone to the tailor for a small piece of work and, when she came back to pick it up, he made advances to her. She had refused him, saying that three pence was not enough for her to become his concubine, that her husband would be angry with her if she did, that the tailor had also made advances to her co-wife who had refused, and that it seemed that he was trying to hurt their husband. The tailor had little to say, except that the woman owed him three pence.

By his time a large group of onlookers had assembled. If anyone present wished, they could question either party; and, if necessary, nearby witnesses could be called. After this, anyone present could give his opinion in the order of seniority, with the younger people speaking first. In this case only adult men gave their opinions, followed by the acting compound head who summed up what had been said as their judgement. However, as he was younger than some of those present, including at least one man from a different compound, he called upon the elders to give the final judgement. This was that the boy who had grabbed the woman had done wrong and would be flogged when he returned home; that the woman was in the right; and that if the tailor made any more trouble they would turn the case over to the authorities, and that in the Native Administration Court he would be liable for a fine. The tailor was grateful for this, and the woman, who had been vindicated, bowed in acknowledgment of her acceptance of the verdict.

In these hearings and in the lower courts the objective is to reach a decision which will be accepted as fair by both parties, so that the dispute will be ended; but if this does not happen, either party may appeal to one of the higher courts. The hearing of cases within the compound is similarly informal, but that of the chiefs' courts was less so, with a summons fee of ten shillings, the calling of all known witnesses, and the imposition of fines and physical punishment on the guilty.

Oaths (imulẹ) and ordeals (aje) are employed to determine guilt when the evidence is contradictory. A plaintiff may be made to swear by Ogun, the God of Iron, touching his tongue to an iron object while asking to die if he is not telling the truth, or to drink from the ground at the Ogboni house while swearing on the earth. Ordeals are of various kinds, not all of which are swallowed. The most famous ordeal, the drinking of *Erythrophleum guineense* or sasswood (ọbọ), was used only for women accused of witchcraft, but witches were rarely brought to trial; usually they were executed secretly by the Egungun or Oro cults. The sasswood ordeal has been outlawed, and both the practice of witchcraft and accusations of witchcraft are now illegal; but oaths by Ogun are recognized in the Native Administration Courts as equivalent to swearing on the Koran or the Bible.

Murder, treason, and burglary were formerly punished by execution, or the guilty were used as human sacrifices. Accidental or provoked manslaughter and assault were punished by fines whose amount depended upon the degree of negligence, provocation, and damage; or a person guilty of assault could be flogged. The hands of some thieves were cut off, others were shackled and made to cut weeds under the supervision of the Ogungbẹ, or they were imprisoned until their family paid heavy fines; sometimes they "sold" (itajẹ) the family by making them pay more and more money each time they came to beg for the prisoner's release until they ran into debt. Rape, seduction, and adultery were punished by fines (oji).

Legislation was far less important than adjudication, as behavior was largely regulated by customary laws of long standing. However, if a song of ridicule which was likely to lead to a disturbance of the peace was to be prohibited, if hours for opening and closing the town gates were to be changed, or if maximum prices for palm wine or maximum expenses for club meetings were to be set, the town and palace chiefs discussed it at one of the meetings in the Ogboni house. If they agreed, Lọwa or an Ẹmẹsẹ was sent to inform the Ọni and, if he agreed, he notified them and they sent a gong beater about town announcing the new regulation. If the Ọni disagreed, the matter was dropped.

During the colonial period, criminal law was modified to conform to British standards of justice, but civil law is still based largely on Yoruba customary law. The kings no longer have the authority to execute murderers, and treason to the kings and burglary are no longer capital offenses. Thieves cannot be punished by cutting off their hands, but prisoners are still made to cut weeds, under the supervision of the Native Administration police.

Native Administration Courts of varying grades of competence were established in the larger towns, with the judges in Ifẹ being drawn from a panel of town and palace chiefs, and written records being kept by a Court Clerk. Much of their time is devoted to the settlement of divorce cases and the determination of how much must be paid to the husband as a refund of the bridewealth and other gifts made at the time of marriage. In one case a woman, who had been sleeping with a lover, had brought suit for divorce. Anyone who had anything to say could speak on the case, including both parties, the clerk, the police, the spectators, and the judges—in this case four palace chiefs. The woman's father spoke against her, which was not unusual as parents often sent their daughters back to their husbands, and in this case she had admitted her infidelity. Moreover, he pointed out that she had only two more months to complete her training in Islam. Many others spoke against her, including the head of the Muslim community. No one spoke for the woman, and she herself said very little. When everyone had been heard, one of the judges left to confer with the Ọni, and when he returned he announced the court's decision: the divorce was granted. This caused a stir, because in earlier times a woman would not usually have been granted a divorce when her father opposed it. The involved discussion of the return of the bridewealth and other gifts ensued.

Magistrates preside over the higher courts in which lawyers appear with their clients, and large sums of money are spent on land cases which could not have been appealed in earlier times. The authority of the Ọni and his chiefs was weakened by the right of appeal to higher courts or to go over their heads to the District Officer; but the people of Ifẹ came to recognize that while the Ọni remains in office until he dies, District Officers were changed frequently because of the policy of reassigning them to different posts, and the views of a new District Officer might differ from those of his predecessor. Because the kings were paid salaries by the government and their appointment was made subject to governmental approval, they became suspect of being tools of the colonial administration in the eyes of some younger, educated men.

Before Nigeria became independent the councils of chiefs were expanded to represent the untitled educated group. These town councils were responsible for the collection of a graduated head tax, part of which remained in their control for local salaries and public works. The national elections and party politics preceding independence markedly affected the climate of Yoruba political life. Unlike the Hausa and the Igbo, the two other major ethnic groups in Nigeria, the Yoruba were deeply divided in their political allegiance between two parties, the AG or Action Group and the NCNC or National Council of Nigeria and the Cameroons. As a result, and because the Hausa and Igbo formed a coalition, they were in a completely subordinate position when independence came.

5

Social Structure

The Clan

YORUBA KINSHIP IS BILATERAL IN THEORY, with incest taboos and kinship terminology extended to known relatives through both male and female relatives, but in practice it is strongly patrilineal. The importance of bilateral relationships is restricted because they depend upon the ability to trace them through all the connecting relatives, and few Yoruba can remember their genealogies for more than four generations back. In contrast, patrilineal descent, in which only male ancestors are counted, is institutionalized in the clan and does not depend upon individual memory.

Every Yoruba is born into a patrilineal clan (idile) whose members are descended from a remote common ancestor. Even when genealogical relations to the clan founder (orisun) or to other clan members have long been forgotten, they are presumed on the basis of membership in the clan, of the common clan names, taboos, and facial marks, of the rights to property and titles which clan members share, and of the reciprocal privileges and obligations which unite them. An individual accepts all members of his own clan as blood relatives, even if he does not know in what way they are actually related; marriage with any of them is as strongly prohibited as it is with the mother's mother's daughter's daughter, where the genealogical ties are completely known. Both sons and daughters are born into the clan of their father, rather than that of the mother; and the children of a man's son belong to his clan, whereas those of his daughter belong to the clan of her husband.

Marriage is patrilocal, with the bride generally coming to live in one of the many rooms in the compound of the groom's father. Matrilocal residence occurs, as when a poor man marries a woman from a wealthy and powerful family, but it is not common. A man who lives with his wife's family is ridiculed for being lazy, and he has much less control of his wife and children, and much less to say about family affairs than in the patrilocal situation. Not only can his wife count on the support of her clan while he is removed from his own clansmen, but his position is weakened because he has failed to fulfill one of the obligations of a husband, that of providing housing for his family. Moreover, matrilocal residence is not a favorable situation for a man to acquire plural wives because they would be much more subject to the first wife's control than if they were living in the husband's compound. The clan is thus a residential grouping whose male members generally live together as a unit until death, and whose female members live with them until marriage.

Even where the clan is too large to be accommodated in a single compound (ile), which may contain several hundred people, segments of the clan are still residential units. A large clan may have a "flock of houses" (agbo ile) or a collectivity of compounds scattered in different parts of town, each occupied by a sub-clan. In such cases an individual belongs both to the sub-clan of the compound into which he was born and to the clan as a whole, symbolized by the original compound from which the others split off.

The clan or the sub-clan is a corporate group, owning the compound in which it dwells, the land on which the compound stands, and farm land outside of town, as well as intangible property such as titles to political and religious offices. It is a self-perpetuating unit, as it includes the dead who may be reborn into the clan, as well as the living. Internally its members are stratified in terms of seniority, sex, and achieved status, but viewed from the outside the members of the same clan are social equivalents.

Clan names (orilẹ) are derived from the personal names of ancestors in Ifẹ and Ilesha, and are usually paired with one name for males and another for females. Not infrequently there are two to four pairs of clan names within the same compound, distinguishing different branches of the clan. This is often explained as due to intermarriage, as when a proud woman insisted on giving her own clan names to her own children because she disliked her senior co-wife. In Ọyọ there are single clan names of a totemic nature, such as Elephant (erin), Ram (agbo), and Rain (ojo). In addition clans also own longer praise names (oriki).

Clan members also wear the same pattern of facial scarification (ila), although members of the Ọni's clan have no facial marks. The number of these clan marks is limited, so that the same pattern is used by unrelated clans. In Ọyọ it is not unusual for women of the royal clan to give their clan mark to their children, and their husbands as commoners are powerless to stop them. In such cases the children are adopted into the royal clan, but they are not normally eligible to become king or to take other titles belonging to the royal clan. Also, if a man has many children he may show his affection toward his wife by giving her one of her daughters to be given the marks of her clan; and again the daughter becomes a member of her mother's clan. Facial marks, which are not unpleasant, are passing out of fashion.

Clan members are spoken of as "children of the house" (ọmọ ile) with males distinguished as "sons of the house" (ọmọ ọkunrin ile) from the females or "daughters of the house" (ọmọ obinrin ile). All clan members, male and female, are considered to be blood relatives (ẹbi, ibatan). The females live in the compound of their birth until they marry, when they go to live with their husbands. The males constitute the stable nucleus of the compound, being born, married, and buried in it. In addition, the compound houses the wives of the male clan members or the "wives of the house" (aya ile). Except for their own children, they are related to the other members of the clan into which they marry as affinal relatives (aya). Finally in many compounds there are outsiders or "strangers" (alejo) who are not related to anyone in the compound, perhaps having come from another town. Some of these are permitted to settle permanently in the compound, marrying and raising families whose males may continue to reside in it; they are counted among the "people of the house" (ara ile), but not as relatives.

The clan and the sub-clan are each headed by its eldest male member, known as the Bale or "father of the house" (baba ile), a term which also refers to a husband as the head of his own family. No one except a male member of the clan can hold this position, and it follows according to strict seniority. Regardless of his chronological age, the eldest male clan member of the compound is always its Bale. If the Bale is incompetent or otherwise unable to serve, he retains his title even if another elder is appointed to perform his functions.

The Bale serves as the principal judge of the compound, presiding when disputes are brought before him, but cases are heard by all the elders and by any other members of the compound who may be present. If a titled chief lives in the compound he is also responsible for settling disputes. A husband is responsible for settling quarrels within his own family; but if he is unsuccessful or if an argument involves members of two different families within the compound, it is referred to the Bale. Any cases which he cannot settle may be referred to the town chiefs, but every effort is made to reach a peaceful settlement within the compound.

A common oath, administered by the Bale in cases involving accusations of the use of bad medicine against a brother or half-brother or of sexual relations with his wife, involves simply the eating of a section of kola nut in the compound's "first chamber" after saying "May the ancestors kill me (if I am guilty)." This oath is considered even more dangerous than the public oaths by Ogun.

The Bale is also responsible for assigning living quarters within the compound, administering clan farmlands assigned to the compound, sacrificing to the founder whose name the compound bears, seeing that the compound is kept in good repair by the adult males, and making medicines and atonements to keep its inhabitants in good health and at peace.

The hierarchy within the clan, based on seniority, runs from the eldest Bale of its several compounds down to the youngest child, and is very important in regulating conduct between the members of the collectivity. Each person is "elder" (agba) to all others born or married into the clan after him. The reciprocal obligations involve authority on the one hand, and deference and respect on the other. Males are seated and served according to their relative seniority, and elders can take larger and choicer portions of what is served. This right, to which juniors cannot object, is spoken of as ireje which is usually translated as "cheating"; however, it is actually the accepted prerogative of elders by virtue of their seniority. The same rights are associated with political office.

In terms of seniority or age, the male clan members of the compound are divided into three groups: the elders (agba ile), the adult males who are economically independent (isọgan), and the young men and boys who are still economically dependent on their fathers and who are referred to as "children of the house" (ọmọ ile). Each group is headed by its senior member, the elders by the Bale, the adults by the Logun (Ologun) which is a military title meaning "Warrior," and the "children" by the Lẹwẹrẹ. The Logun is the executive and administrator for the Bale, charged with overseeing the work done by the adult males for the Bale and for the king. When the king wanted a new road made or the palace walls or roof repaired, he sent to the Bale who had the Logun assemble his men for the task. The Bale also tells the Logun to have the compound or the street in front of it repaired. The Logun and the adult males are also responsible for the burial of members of the sub-clan.

When a new Logun is appointed, all those senior to him automatically join the elders of the compound. The new Logun selects and begins to train a younger man as his own successor. He chooses a young man whom he considers to be good for the position because he is smart and able to keep the other young men—particularly his juniors—in order, and to command their respect and obedience. The age of the successor is not important, except that he must have achieved economic independence from his father and thus be a member of the group which the Logun heads. He may be as young as twenty years if he is the smartest and ablest. The training of the successor continues until the Logun feels he is too old to carry on his active duties and resigns from his position.

In Ifẹ each compound has a special large room for the Bale, known as the "first chamber" (akodi ọkankan). When a man succeeds as Bale he moves from his former quarters to this chamber where much of its important business is transacted. In it, sacrifices are offered, the Bale hears and judges disputes between members of the compound, and the elders, adult males, and wives of the compound hold their separate monthly or bimonthly meetings (ipade). The Logun presides over the meetings of the adult men, which may be held in his own quarters if it is large enough to accommodate them. The adult men and the elders may meet together to eat and discuss the affairs of the compound, such as forthcoming sacrifices, repairs to the compound, the allocation of clan farm land, and the collection of taxes. When an important matter is to be discussed, clan members meet in the first chamber of the original compound with the senior Bale of the various compounds presiding.

The wives of the male clan members of the compound also hold bimonthly meetings in the main chamber of the compound, and one of their main functions is the cleaning of this chamber and the rubbing of its walls with dung. This group is headed by the "mother of the house" or Iyale (iya ile) a term which is also applied to the senior wife in a polygynous family. She need not be the eldest wife; rather her seniority is based on the fact that she has been married into the compound longer than any of the others. The Iyale settles quarrels between the wives, advises them in the care of their children, and organizes the preparation of food when a feast is planned for the whole compound.

The female members of the sub-clan hold bimonthly meetings in the private quarters of one of their number who serves as hostess. A married woman may return to the household of her birth for this purpose, or she may invite the group to meet in the compound of her husband. These meetings are headed by the senior female clan member of the compound.

The clan and sub-clan are fundamental to the structure of city government. Compounds headed by Bale are grouped into precincts headed by precinct chiefs; these are organized into the five wards of Ifẹ, each headed by a ward chief and with the precinct chiefs serving on his council; the wards in turn comprise the city of Ifẹ ruled by the Ọni, with the ward chiefs serving with three others as his town chiefs.

The Family

The clan and sub-clan completely overshadow the immediate family in importance. The immediate family consisting of a man, his wives, and their children is of less significance and is known only by a descriptive name referring to the dwelling which it occupies, "my house" (ile mi), or, to distinguish it from the compound, "house that of mine" (ile ti emi). Informants explained the lack of emphasis on the immediate family as due, in part at least, to its instability as con- trasted to the permanent nature of the clan. As one man put it, "Wives can come and go, and after divorce one has nothing to do with them; but one can never change his consanguinal relatives." When informants saw photographs of King George VI of England with his wife and two daughters captioned "The King and His Family," they were at first deeply shocked that such an important man should have so small a family. Later, when it was explained that in a sense we include other relatives, they were highly amused by our idea of what constitutes a family.

The sub-family, consisting of a wife and her children in a polygynous family, is perhaps more important than the immediate family. They have a room in the husband's house to themselves, and they share possessions in common. When they are young, children of co-wives play together on the best of terms, but as they grow older and property rights become important, they usually grow apart because of quarrels over possessions. When the father dies, his personal property is divided into approximately equal shares according to the number of his wives who have children, regardless of the number of children each wife has, except that a wife who has no children may receive only a nominal share to provide for her until she can remarry. Essentially it is the children, and not the wives, who inherit, and the eldest child of each wife takes one share in the name of all the children of his mother. He may keep and use this heritage as he sees fit; but he is held responsible for the economic welfare of the others. Also, in any dispute a person will, in the words of a proverb, "take his mother's side" against his father's other wives, and even against his father. The sub-family is known as a "corner" (origun), a term which applies also to the lineal descendants of a grandmother or a great-grand- mother.

Institutionalized Friendship

Kinship is the basic factor in the social structure, but not all social units are based on it. Institutionalized friendship may, or may not, cut across kinship lines. A best friend is referred to as "friend not-see-not-sleep" (ọrẹ ko-ri-ko-sun), meaning that one does not go to sleep without having seen his best friend. Through experience one learns whose advice he can rely upon and whom he can trust not to reveal confidences, both of which are important to the role of a best friend. In time of trouble one goes to his best friend even before turning to his mother, and he confides in him things he would not tell his clansmen. He tells his best friend what is to be done at his burial and how he wishes his property to be divided, and at his death his best friend is called by his family to learn his last wishes. Before writing was introduced, the best friend provided a means by which one could leave his last will and testament.

Institutionalized friendship often begins with a fight, and a reconciliation, between two boys when they are about eight to twelve years old. One man, as a young boy, had gone hunting rats with a group of other boys. He had no axe, so he helped a younger boy who had one to dig out a rat hole, knowing that they should share the kill equally. Five rats were killed and they started to fight over who was to take the fifth rat. The elder boy beat the younger one into submission, and then took only two rats as his share. They became friends (ọrẹ), the friendship ripened over the years, and eventually they became best friends. Women also have best friends, but this seldom lasts; in part, because they are physically separated when they marry, and in part, because, according to men, women cannot keep a secret.

The following legend about two best friends was recorded in Ifẹ and, in a slightly different form, in Igana.

Once there were two men who were best friends. One of them had a fight with another man and killed him. Escaping, he ran to the house of his friend and told him what had happened. He said that the king would arrest and punish him. His friend advised him to act like a crazy man, to dress in rags and, when questioned, to speak nothing but nonsense. And his friend made a fire and put a pot of medicine of leaves and water on it.

When the king sent for the man, he did as he had been told. He spoke only meaningless sounds and did not answer questions coherently. His friend testified that the man was insane and that he had been keeping him in his back yard for thirty days, giving him medicine for his ailment. The king said that this crazy man could not have been the one who killed the other man, and set him free.

Seven months passed, and the friend asked him, "Which is greater, a man's mother or his best friend?" He replied, "His mother." His friend said, "Then tell your mother what you have done." So he went to his mother and, taking her into her room, told her secretly that he was the one who had killed that man seven months before. When his mother heard this she cried, "My head!!" She ran straight to the king and said, "Please, your Majesty, it was my son who killed that man," and she began to beg the king to pardon her son.

Meanwhile her son ran back to his best friend and told him what had happened, asking him again for help. His friend told him to admit the killing. When he was called before the king and accused of killing the man he answered, "Yes, I killed him. And I killed your father too. And I killed the man who died yesterday. And I am going to kill so-and-so tomorrow." When the king heard this he said, "This man really is crazy. Take him away."

When he went back to his friend to thank him, his friend repeated his question, "Which is greater, a man's mother or his best friend?" Without hesitation he replied, "Now I know truly, the greater is his best friend."

Later his friend died, and he mourned him constantly. After a while another man came to him, asking to become his best friend; but he refused, saying that no one could be as faithful to him as the man who had twice saved his life. The other replied, "But I can show you I love you as much as he did. I can be an even better friend than he was." The man asked for time to think it over, and the next day he went hunting and killed an antelope. He dug a grave and buried it like a man.

Then he ran to the new friend and told him that while he was hunting he had accidentally killed a man, and that he had buried him. He took him to the place and showed him the grave. When they parted the new friend ran to the king and said, "This man that I have tried to befriend, he really kills men. He must have killed that other man before. Just today he has killed a man and buried him, and I have seen the grave."

The king said, "What? Lead me to the grave." So they seized the accused and all went with the king into the forest. When they dug up the grave, they found the body of the antelope. The false friend was exposed, and the man never took another friend.

Clubs

The second institution which cuts across kinship lines is the club (ẹgbẹ), of which there were several hundred in Ifẹ in 1937. These also may grow out of childhood associations. When his clan is performing a religious festival, or when he is sacrificing to his ancestral guardian soul, a child may invite his playmates and their friends to come to eat with him; and he may be invited by them in return. If this continues, they choose a name for their club and invite an elder man and an elder woman to serve in an advisory capacity as "father of the club" and "mother of the club." Because of the manner in which they are formed, the members of a club are of about the same age, and there are societies of children, adults, and elderly people of both sexes; but in Ifẹ, at least, they are not age sets or age grades of the type found in some African societies, and as reported for the Ekiti Yoruba. A man can invite the members of his club to his feast when he is performing a festival and to go about town accompanied by a drummer that day. One's social position is judged by the number of his followers on such occasions, as well as by their wealth and social status. Before the introduction of cocoa, the clubs also formed working bees when invited by one of their members.

Since the introduction of cocoa, the clubs have become essentially social societies, and several new features have been added. Monthly meetings are held with the members serving as host in turn, entrance fees and dues are collected and recorded by a secretary, and officers are elected by ballot. Societies of Christians contribute money to teachers and ministers in Ifẹ and, when a member dies, they buy the coffin, carry him to the cemetery, dig the grave, and bury him. The cult group is another unit in the society that can cut across kinship lines, but it is primarily religious rather than social in nature.

Kinship Terminology

The basic kinship terms are commonly used both in reference and in address in a classificatory manner, but when more specific information is required they can be used descriptively to express any relationship precisely. Among consanguinal or blood relatives, lineal and collateral relatives are distinguished. Both of these are reckoned bilaterally, through male and female relatives, as widely as the connecting relatives are remembered. Lineal relatives (ẹbi) include one's father (baba) and mother (iya) in the first ascending generation, and one's father's father (baba baba), father's mother (iya baba), mother's father (baba iya), and mother's mother (iya iya). The Yoruba language is characterized by the post-positional genitive, with the object following the possessor, so that "baba iya mi" means "father of mother my" or "my mother's father." One can continue in this fashion to one's father's mother's mother's father (baba iya iya baba) and others in the fourth generation and beyond; but beyond the fourth generation all lineal relatives are known simply as "ancestors" (iran), and actual relationships are rarely remembered. The father's father and mother's mother are also known as grandfather (baba nla, baba agba) and grandmother (iya nla, iya agba).

For lineal descendants the terms are simpler because sex is not usually distinguished, so that there are simply child (ọmọ), grandchild (ọmọ ọmọ), great grandchild (ọmọ ọmọ ọmọ) and great great grandchild (ọmọ ọmọ ọmọ ọmọ). To distinguish the sex of one's child, one simply adds the words "man" (ọkunrin) and "woman" (obinrin), as for son (ọmọ ọkunrin) and daughter (ọmọ obinrin).

Neither is sex distinguished in the terms of reference for collateral relatives (ibatan, ibatọn),[7] but relative age or seniority is. All collateral relatives, regardless of either sex or generation, are referred to as "elder sibling" (ẹgbọn) if they were born before the speaker and as "younger sibling" (aburo) if born after him. These two terms are reciprocal, and except for lineal relatives all members of one's own clan are classed as collateral relatives, even when the actual relationship cannot be traced. Collateral relatives in the first ascending generation are referred to simply as "elder sibling" or "younger sibling," depending on relative age, or more specifically as "my elder (or younger) sibling, elder (or younger) sibling of my father (or mother)" and those in the first descending generation as "younger (or elder) sibling of my child."

All clan mates of one's own generation are referred to as "elder sibling" and "younger sibling," including one's own full and half brothers and sisters. Sex again can be distinguished if necessary, as in "elder brother" (ẹgbọn ọkunrin) and

---

[7] In an earlier publication (Bascom, 1944:10–11), ibatan was defined as "consanguinal relatives," but further field work showed this to be inaccurate; one's parents and four grandparents and all other lineal ancestors are not his ibatan, but their descendants are.

"younger sister" (aburo obinrin). To distinguish one's own full brothers and sisters it is necessary to speak of "my elder (or younger) sibling, child of my father and my mother." This is the usual implication when one says "my elder (or younger) sibling, child of my mother," or more simply "child of my mother," but these phrases may refer to half siblings by a previous marriage. Similarly "child of my father" implies a relationship through co-wives in a polygynous family even though it and the fuller form "my elder (or younger) sibling, child of my father" do not state whether the two individuals have the same, or different mothers. To make these distinctions one may say "child of my father and my mother," "child of my father who is not child of my mother," or "child of my mother who is not child of my father."

Unlike many societies with unilineal descent, no distinction is made between parallel cousins and cross cousins; nor are there any forms of preferred cousin marriage. Both a father's sister's child and a father's brother's child are referred to as "child of the elder (or younger) sibling of my father" or as "my elder (or younger) sibling, child of the elder (or younger) sibling of my father," depending on the brother's or sister's age relative to that of the father. Similarly a mother's brother's child and a mother's sister's child are both referred to as "child of the elder (or younger) sibling of my mother." Neither the sex of the parent's sibling nor that of the cousin is normally distinguished unless a question about it is raised.

In referring to relatives who are not present, one may be as specific as is necessary, depending on the listener's knowledge of and interest in the relationship in question, but commonly the basic kinship terms are used in a classificatory manner. Any ancestor may be spoken of as "father" or "mother." When it is necessary to distinguish one's own biological father and mother from other lineal relatives or from collateral relatives who, out of respect, are addressed as father or mother, one may say "my father" or "my mother" or, more specifically, "father who begat me" or "mother who begat me" (iya ti o bi mi) or "my own father" or "my own mother" (iya mi papa). Similarly one may refer to the child of a collateral relative younger than the speaker either as his "younger sibling" or as his "child." If asked "Is it your own child?" (ọmọ rẹ papa) the speaker may reply in the affirmative or explain the relationship descriptively, for example, "the child of my younger sibling" or "my younger sibling, the child of the child of my father."

In addressing relatives the use of these kinship terms becomes much more classificatory, complex, and subtle. To use the descriptive terms of reference in addressing grandparents is to express contempt for them, showing a lack of the normal respect due them. They are usually addressed as "father" or "mother," and it is said that, in olden times, when fathers were addressed by their personal names, if a child addressed his father as "father," the reply would be, "No. I am not your father. There he is," pointing to the father's father. "Father" and "mother" are also used in address to show respect for a number of consanguineal and affinal relatives, including parents' siblings who are fifteen years or more older than the speaker, the siblings of a wife's mother, and a husband's brothers. They are also used in addressing non-relatives who are only a few years older than the speaker, if their name is not known. If the speaker knew his name he would not address him as "father" unless he were an important chief, or to give insult. One of the insults likely to lead to a fight is a greeting which an individual does not deserve in terms of seniority, wealth, hereditary status, or intimacy. A common insult to Europeans, which they frequently mistake as a compliment, is for a stranger to call out to them in greeting, "my master" (ọga mi).

Sons and daughters are addressed by name. If parents were to address them as "my child" others would think they were boasting about the fact that they have children and would ask, "What is he bragging about? Is he the only person who has any children?" On the other hand if someone is young enough to be a child of the speaker, and his name is not known, he may be addressed as "child," "son," "daughter," "boy," or "girl," even if they are married adults. These are neither terms of affection nor of respect, but simply imply a considerable age differential and the fact that the personal name is unknown.

All collateral relatives older than the speaker may be addressed as "elder sibling," but it is more usual—and more respectful—to address them by name. To show respect for elder siblings of one's own generation, they are addressed by the English terms "brother" (burọda) or "sister" (sista), but in former times they and younger siblings were addressed by name. To show respect for the elder siblings of one's parents, and for those who are only slightly younger, they are addressed as "father" or "mother;" more distant collateral relatives are addressed in this way to show respect only if they are old enough to have children as old as the speaker. Those who are younger than this are addressed as "brother" and "sister" to show respect, as are the younger siblings of one's parents who are older than the speaker. All collateral relatives who are younger than the speaker are addressed by name or as "younger sibling."

Affinal relatives are classified into three major groups, "husbands" (ọkọ), "wives" (aya), and "affines" or "in-laws" (ana). The term "husband" refers to a woman's own husband and all the members of his clan, including female clan members. The term "wife" refers to a man's wives and to all the wives of his clansmen. These two terms are reciprocal, and a woman refers to her husband's sisters as "husband," while they speak of her as their "wife." The term "affine" covers the remaining relatives by marriage: all the members of the clans of a man's wives, excluding his own wives and the wives of his clansmen, and all the men who have married women of one's own clan, excepting a woman's own husband. The term "affine" is also reciprocal in reference, for example between a man's sister's husband and his wife's brother. The three terms are extended bilaterally as far as actual relationships are known.

A man refers to his wives simply as "wife" (aya), or he may speak of the one to whom he has been longest married as his "senior wife" (iyale) and to the others as "junior wife" (iyawo). He may refer to his newest wife as "my little junior wife" (iyawo mi kekere), and to a girl to whom he is engaged as "my junior wife" or "my junior wife of the road" (iyawo mi ọna). Men address their own wives by name, but if a wife has a living child he shows respect and affection by addressing her as "mother of so-and-so," mentioning the child's personal name. A wife must not address her husband by personal name or by nickname. If he has a living child she may address him as "father of so-and-so," but if not she cannot use any form of address; she can only say, "Do you hear?" or something else to catch his attention. In reference, she speaks of her own husband as "father of my house" (bale mi).

Whereas among collateral relatives seniority is simply a matter of relative age, among affinal relatives it is based on the length of affiliation with the clan or sub-clan, whether by birth or by marriage, and the ages of the individuals concerned are not relevant. Thus a woman is senior to all members born into the clan of her husband after her marriage, but junior to those born before it, even if they were born on the day she married. As soon as a boy or girl can talk, he may address any woman who has married into his clan after his birth as "junior wife" (iyawo), even if she is much older and is her husband's first wife or "senior wife" (iyale). However, if a man were to have sexual relations with the wife of an elder brother he would be severely punished, and to have relations with the wife of a younger brother is considered unthinkable.

The wives of any consanguinal relative (lineal or collateral), including those of all male members of one's own clan, may be addressed as "wife," but co-wives of one's mother may be addressed as "mother" if they are senior to the speaker. More often, they and other wives of consanguinal relatives are addressed by name, regardless of seniority, and to show respect they may be addressed as "mother of so-and-so." In reference, wives of consanguinal relatives are spoken of as "my wife" or "my junior wife" or descriptively as "wife of my elder (or younger) sibling," spelling out the specific relationship involved. Co-wives of one's mother may be referred to as "my mother's senior (or junior) wife," depending upon the time of marriage, as "my mother's co-wife" (orogun iya mi), or "my father's "wife" (aya baba mi).

In return a woman refers to all consanguinal relatives of her husband as "husband," regardless of their sex. She may address all those born after her marriage by name, but she must never use the personal Yoruba name in addressing those who are senior to her. For those born shortly before her marriage, she must invent her own nicknames or use their Christian names. If they are old enough to have children, she addresses them as "father (or mother) of so-and-so," using the Yoruba personal name of the child if it was born after her marriage or a nickname or Christian name if the child is her senior. If a man (or woman) has his first child some years after her marriage, and the difference in their seniority is not sufficient to warrant addressing him as "father of so-and-so" she may continue to address him by the nickname she has given him. A woman may refer to and sometimes addresses the female consanguinal relatives of her husband who are members of her own household as "mother of my husband." This is true whether they are older or younger than her husband, and, to show respect, a young girl of eleven may be addressed in this way, although she would not otherwise be addressed or referred to as such. Those who are too young to be called this are spoken of as "child of my husband."

A man addresses his father-in-law and mother-in-law as "father" and "mother." He does not use their name in address, but he may enquire about them by name if they are not present. He addresses his wife's siblings and her parents' siblings by name. To show respect for her mother's siblings, he may address them by the English terms "brother" and "sister," and, to show respect for her father's siblings, if they are older than he is and of good character, he may address them "father" or "mother." Because women marry at an earlier age than men, and because in polygynous families men may take young brides late in life, a son-in-law may be of the same age as his father-in-law. In earlier times a man was expected to prostrate himself before all of his wife's relatives as soon as they were able to talk, but as the result of European contact the relationship between "affines" is losing its former character and becoming more like the relations between consanguinal relatives or simple friends. Some men prostrate themselves at the same time that the husband of one of their relatives is prostrating before them and, if they are younger, they may try to prostrate themselves before he does. Some parents-in-law will not permit their son-in-law to prostrate himself if he is of their age.

A daughter's husband, sister's husband, brother's daughter's husband, or the husband of any consanguinal relative is addressed by name. To show respect, he may be addressed as "father of so-and-so" if he has a child, but a father-in-law is unlikely to do so unless they are about the same age and see each other frequently. If they are of similar age and have become good friends, a father-in-law may address his daughter's husband as "my partner" (awe mi), and be so addressed in return. If a daughter's husband were addressed as "my affine" (ana mi), he would carefully consider the tone of voice to see whether any disrespect were intended.

Seniority, based upon the time of marriage, is also important in relations between co-wives within the polygynous family and among the wives of the compound as a whole. Each woman is the junior wife (iyawo) of all those married into the clan before her, and the senior wife (iyale) of those married after her regardless of their relative ages. A woman must be careful to express proper respect for her senior co-wives in the forms of address she uses for them, as failure to do so can lead to serious quarrels and even to divorce. A woman may address her junior co-wives by personal name, but this is not respectful enough for her seniors. The most respectful form of address for a senior wife is "my mother" (iya mi). A second wife addresses the first wife in this way if the senior wife is much older and has been married much longer, and all subsequent wives use this form of address to the first wife regardless of their relative ages and seniority. Where the relations to a senior wife do not call for so much respect, she may be addressed as "mother of so-and-so," mentioning the nickname of the child if he was born before the speaker married, or his personal name if he was born afterwards and is junior to the speaker. If the senior wife has no child, she may be addressed as "mother of such-and-such," mentioning the name of the ward in which she was born; or, with about the same degree of respect, she may be addressed as "my senior wife."

A woman may address any of her junior co-wives by personal name, including the most recently married, who may also be addressed as "junior wife." If a junior wife has a child, she is usually addressed as "mother of so-and-so," using the real name of the child, implying friendship and respect; nicknames are unnecessary because the senior wife would always be married before her junior wife's child by their husband is born. If a senior wife wishes to show respect and affection

for a junior wife who has no child, she may address her as "my partner" regardless
of differences in their ages and seniority; however the junior wife could not use
this form of address in return unless they were nearly the same age and had married
at about the same time. This form of address might be used reciprocally between
the first and second wife, or the fourth and the fifth, but not by the first and fifth.
Its usage is not common, and it depends upon the affection of the senior wife for
her junior co-wife; but the relationships between co-wives are expressed in a
delicate choice of forms of address which show varying degrees of affection and
respect for seniority.

Yoruba kinship terminology stresses the factor of seniority, including
relative age as one of its manifestations, which is so important in relationships
between members of the clan and inhabitants of the same compound. Generation
is an important factor in the classification of lineal relatives, but it is subordinate
to seniority in the case of collateral relatives who are simply junior or senior. A
clear distinction is drawn between these two categories of consanguinal relatives,
which are also distinguished from affinal relatives. Sex is of relatively little importance, being used only to distinguish "father" and "mother" and the new terms
for elder siblings, "brother" and "sister"; on the other hand the same term refers
to a woman's husband and to his sister. The threefold classification of affinal relatives distinguishes the members of the husband's clan (ọkọ), the wives who have
married into it (aya), and all other affines (ana) who live outside the compound.
Finally, the kinship terminology provides a subtle means of expressing delicate
shades of respect, affection, and supplication, or their reverse. The forms of address
which express respect may be used because of the individual's seniority, title, or
good character; they are also used to express a special degree of affection and intimacy, or when requesting a special favor, or begging forgiveness for an offense.

6

The Life Cycle

Birth and Childcare

WHEN A CHILD IS BORN it is sprinkled with water to make it cry. No word is spoken until it does, to prevent it from becoming impotent or barren. No one younger than the mother should be present; in Ifẹ it is believed that delivery would be delayed if the husband were present, but a male doctor may be called in if there are difficulties. If it is the mother's first child, it is taken to the back yard where the umbilical cord is bound tightly with thread and then cut, using a knife from the midrib of a leaf of the bamboo palm or a piece of glass, as a metal knife is believed to cause stomach ache. This is done by an elderly woman attendant and should not be done by a man. The placenta is buried in the back yard by a woman, in a hole dug by men and filled in with stones. On this spot the child is bathed with a loofah sponge and rubbed with palm oil. The mother is present if she is able, but she must not speak until the bath has been completed. The child is held by the feet and given three shakes to make it strong and brave, so that it will not be afraid of falling or of noises, and so that it will not have spasms; its head is touched gently to the ground so that later it will not hurt itself when it falls down.

The attendant carries the child back to the house with the mother following, and when the mother has been seated on a mat the attendant calls her three times by name. When the mother responds on the third time the attendant hands her the child saying, "Take your child." If the mother has had other children the cutting of the cord and the bath are done in the room, and the mother may speak before the child is bathed. A fire is built to keep the room warm, and, after the mother has bathed, many people come to see the baby and to congratulate the mother on her safe delivery, bringing presents of food or money.

Many children are given special names according to the circumstances of their birth. Thus the first-born twin, who is considered younger because he was sent ahead by the other, is called Taiwo, meaning that he came to inspect the world for the senior twin, called Kẹhinde, meaning that he arrived afterwards.

There are special names for the first, second, third, and fourth children born after twins, for children born with the umbilical cord around their neck, for children born in an unruptured caul, for children born face down, for children born with six fingers, and for other circumstances of birth.

The mother and the child remain in the house for a specified period of time, usually six days for girls and eight days for boys, but the period varies from clan to clan. On this day the child is named and it is taken out of the house for the first time since the day of its birth. Early in the morning the child is bathed, and the mother bathes, dresses in fine clothes, and sits with her child near a bowl of water. The father comes forward and drops money into the water, announcing his name for the child, followed by his father and mother. Then the mother names the child without contributing any money. Then the father's relatives who have come to greet the child, followed by others present, drop small amounts of money into the water, each suggesting whatever name they like for the child. Children receive many names at this time, and each person may address the child by the name he has given it; but in the course of time most of these names are forgotten while the one most commonly used becomes established through repeated usage. This is the name which the father and mother like best and is often the name suggested by one of them in the first place. A relative would be ashamed to suggest a name without contributing money, but even a small child may do so if he contributes. Some individuals suggest several names when they drop money into the water, and others suggest none. Many Yoruba names begin with the name of the deity which the individual worships, for example, 'Fagbemi, meaning "Ifa helps me." If a child has a name because of special circumstances of its birth, for example a twin, no new names are suggested; the relatives simply say, "Kehinde (or Taiwo), here is your money" as they drop it in the water. The money is kept by the mother to buy food for the child, or, perhaps, a chicken or goat for it to raise.

Kola nuts, small bits of dried meat, and pieces of raw yam are arranged in groups, containing one of each, on a calabash which is passed to the relatives present, each one taking one of the groups. After this a large feast is prepared in honor of the child, who is considered to be the guest. Some of the yams and meat are fed to the child, so that when it is old enough to eat it will be able to say "This is what I met in the world"; and if a child misbehaves in later years, its parents can reproach it by asking, "Did you help to plant the yams that you ate on the day you were named?" On this day also the child's head is shaved for the first time and its hair is saved to make a charm to keep it in good health; also, the father gives the mother a large cloth for the child to sleep in.

Circumcision and excision are normally performed in the first month, and the cutting of the facial marks (ila) follows about two months later, after the wound has healed. If the child is an abiku, "one born to die" (see p. 74), circumcision or excision is postponed until after it has passed the age at which it "had died before," and it is given its facial marks on the same day. Both circumcision and excision are individual affairs, and not the basis of initiation rites as they are in many African societies. Christians and Muslims are giving up facial marks, but boys must still be circumcised and girls excised before marriage. It is shameful for a man to be uncircumcised, and it is believed that a child will die if its head touches its mother's clitoris during childbirth.

Infants are nursed or given cool water to drink whenever they cry. Starting after the naming ceremony, or sometimes earlier, children are given a purgative to drink early each morning which may or may not contain reserpine.[8] This continues until they are about six months old and the first tooth appears, when they are fed cornstarch gruel or porridge. Children are given small portions of adult food as soon as they ask for it, but they continue nursing until they are two to four years old, when they are weaned by refusing the breast or rubbing it with bitter leaf (*Vernonia amygdalina*). Bottle feeding became popular among educated Yoruba only after World War II, and formerly it was believed that a child would die if it was weaned before two years of age. Until a child is weaned the mother avoids sexual relations because of the belief that pregnancy will spoil her milk and cause the child to have diarrhea, and that the health of the child in her womb will also be impaired. Women are described as being more interested in their new child· than in sex at this time, and in polygynous families the husbands have other wives. Until a child can walk it is carried on the mother's back beneath a cloth sash tied across her breast. Even when they have passed the age of five, children are carried in this way when they become tired on the way to market or to the farm.

Childhood and Education

By the time a child is five it is already imitating the activities of its parents, perhaps picking up the broom and sweeping the street with no purpose and without being asked, or, if the father is a tailor, pretending to crank a box which represents the hand-operated sewing machine. If the mother sells porridge in the market, the daughter may pretend to grind corn, rubbing a stone back and forth on the ground. Or a girl may put an empty calabash on her head and go about calling out that she is selling cloths; another child may call back, "Cloth seller, come here," and then bargain for her wares, paying for the imaginary cloth with pieces of broken china. Imitative play of this type is more or less tolerated and ignored unless children get in the way or are destructive. If a carpenter finds his son trying to fasten two pieces of wood together using nails from his work box, and a stone for a hammer, he is far less apt to encourage him at this stage than to say, "Don't spoil those nails!"

Children are very imaginative in devising new games and playing at new occupations which have developed since European contact. The two daughters and son of an interpreter, aged five, six, and eight, played at their father's activities as a letter writer. Taking a pencil and an old piece of paper, the elder daughter asked her brother, "What is your name?" and he answered, "Bisi." She then made a

---

[8] One recipe for the purgative (agbo) calls for ewe asofeiyẹjẹ (*Rauwolfia vomitoria* leaves), ewe efinrin (*Ocimum spp.* leaves), ewe ẹruju (*Uvaria chamae* leaves), ewe otili (*Cajanus cajan* leaves), and ẹru awonka (probably *Xylopia aethiopica*). *Rauwolfia,* which is the source of reserpine, was introduced into Western medicine as a treatment for hypertension in 1949. It is also used by Yoruba doctors who specialize in psychiatric disorders to induce sleep in their patients.

scribbled line on the paper and asked, "How much do you owe?" He replied, "Ten pounds," and she scribbled another line. She asked, "To whom do you owe it?" and he replied, "To Layẹmi" and she scribbled again. Then she imitated type-writing, bouncing her hands up and down on the paper with her fingers spread far apart. Then she took Bisi's thumb and rolled it on the paper as if taking his fingerprint, which is necessary to make such documents legal.

During my work with their father these three children invented a new game, playing anthropologist. One sat in my chair on my cushion, with paper and pencil in hand. The second sat in their father's chair, acting as "interpreter," while the third sat on a bench as the informant customarily did. The second child turned to the first and said, "You are my master," and then to the third child, saying in Yoruba, "The white man wants you to tell about Odua." The third child replied in Yoruba and the second turned to the first and "interpreted," making a series of meaningless sounds which were supposed to sound like English. The first child scribbled on the paper, and replied with more nonsense syllables and the second child turned to the third with a new question in Yoruba. When the game became boring, the first child stood up and stretched, saying (in nonsense syllables) "Come, let us go," and the other two children got up. The first child pretended to put on a sun helmet, stood in front of the house with his hands on his hips, and then pretended to ride off on a bicycle. When caught playing their new game, all three scampered away.

When children are five or six years old they are encouraged to participate, to the extent that they are able, in whatever work the parent of the same sex is doing; no pressure is necessary because for children this is simply an extension of the games they have devised for themselves and it brings them close to the parent. A girl who accompanies her mother to the stream to do laundry is given a small piece of cloth to wash. When the mother brings water home, she is given a small calabash to carry water in on her head, steadying it with both hands, while her mother carries a bucketful. If the load is too heavy, the mother may pour out some water and let her carry the almost empty calabash. The parents are more concerned that the child does not attempt more than it can accomplish, than in the possibility that the child may make mistakes, or fail. But for the child it is an important matter, and it is touching to see the serious determination of a young girl struggling up a hill with water trickling down her face, or the hot tears of a girl whose wares and few coins have been knocked from her head and scattered in the market. Mothers are respon-sible for teaching their own trade to their daughters, so that they too may have their own income after marriage. Boys are taught farming by their fathers and may also learn a trade from their father or as an apprentice.

Yoruba education stresses economic and psychological independence, but not social independence. The child learns to respect the bonds of kinship, to perform economic activities, to watch out for his own interests, and to make decisions for himself. From the beginning of imitative play there is a gradual transition to the adult activities which the child will perform throughout the rest of his life. How-ever, this has also changed as the result of European contact, with increasing numbers of children going to school, where they are placed in an artificial environ-ment and assigned tasks which may be unrelated to what they later do as adults.

Betrothal and Marriage

Girls were generally betrothed before puberty in former times, often at five years of age; and sometimes they were promised to a close friend of the father before they were born. Usually, however, a man negotiates through an intermediary, a clansman or friend or even a wife, and can not approach either a girl or her parents to propose marriage. The proposal is not accepted immediately, and usually the intermediaries have to return several times before they receive an answer, while the girl's parents are making careful inquiries into the character of their prospective son-in-law. If they approve of the man, they consult a diviner, accompanied by the intermediary, to learn whether the marriage will lead to trouble or whether their daughter will have children and prosper in the marriage. If the prognostication is good, the groom is responsible for the sacrifices prescribed; if it is bad, the proposal is refused. It is extremely rude to refuse an offer of marriage under other circumstances, and if the suitor is not acceptable, the parents resort to a subterfuge which demonstrates the faith in Ifa divination. Instead of stating, "She will have children" they whisper so that they cannot be heard, "The sun will not rise tomorrow," confident that this proposal will be rejected. A proverb refers to such subterfuges: "As they have wisdom in the house of the intermediary, even so are they wise in the house of those who give their child in marriage." With increasing mobility and more children attending school and college, these steps are sometimes omitted and couples marry without parental consent.

If the suitor is approved, the intermediary is told to have him come, so that the girl's family can meet him. The suitor goes with a male friend or relative and, if they wish to come, his parents and his intermediary; he is told to bring the first installment of the bridewealth to seal the engagement. This is known as "becoming in-laws" (idana) and henceforth the man refers to the girl as his fiancée or "junior wife of the road" and she refers to him as her "husband." In Ifẹ this installment consisted of five yams, five kola nuts, and two logs of firewood from the ita tree (*Celtis spp.*); but it has been divided into two gifts and has increased in value. When marriage is first proposed, the intermediary takes forty kola nuts and ten shillings to the girl's father, and the yams and firewood are given when the engagement is sealed.

The second installment, known as "love money" can be given at any time before the third year after puberty, when the girl becomes "marriageable." It formerly consisted of cowry shells equivalent to two shillings six pence, of which three pence or six pence were used to buy a cloth for the girl to wear, and the rest was divided between the mother, the father, and their relatives. In 1937 this payment could run as high as five pounds.

The final installment, made just before marriage, is known as "wife money." This was also two shillings six pence in the last century, of which six pence went to the mother, six tenths of a penny went to the father, and the balance was spent to buy clothes and other things for the bride. By 1937 this had become the principal payment, running as high as seven pounds ten shillings.

In addition to bridewealth a suitor gives many other gifts during the lengthy engagement. The gifts in cash in the last century totalled only five shillings, but even an elderly informant could not personally remember a marriage which cost less than fifteen shillings. By 1937 gifts in cash had risen to thirteen pounds, and the total expenses of marriage ran as high as fifty pounds and more. Since then they have risen even higher. A father is expected to provide the bridewealth for the first wife of each of his sons.

The first function of bridewealth is to preserve the marriage. As the Yoruba themselves say, it is given to keep the wife in her husband's house; otherwise she would have affairs with other men and the marriage would not last. They add that it also serves as a bond to insure that the husband will not mistreat his wife, because if this can be proved in court, he cannot collect as much at the time of divorce. Thus it serves the interest of both the husband and wife. Some Yoruba consider it as a recompense to the parents for the loss of the future services of their daughter; but others deny this, saying that every woman should start to work for herself when she is old enough, and besides, every woman should have a husband. Some consider it as compensation for the mother's care of her daughter; but others point out that it is too small to be adequate for this. As we shall see later in this chapter, it operates to reserve wives for older men. Finally, bridewealth established the husband as the legal father of the wife's children, regardless of whom the biological father may be. As a proverb says, "One who does not own a kola tree cannot have its fruit" (Eni ti ko ni igi obi ki ini eso). However in recent years it has been possible for the biological father to claim the child by the payment of a fixed fee. Even in earlier times the payment of bridewealth did *not* mean that women were chattel purchased in the market like goats or sheep or slaves; they could sue for divorce, own their own property, and even sue their husband if he willfully destroyed it.

Traditional marriage customs were still observed by conservative families in 1937, but various elements were omitted or modified depending on the wealth, education, and religion of the bride and groom. It is not possible to discuss all of these variations here, but some of the changes will be noted in describing the older customs, as observed in the nineteenth century, after which the newer patterns will be mentioned briefly.

As soon as the engagement was sealed, a man had the right to collect damages (oji) for adultery if his wife proved unfaithful. If there was a child, he could claim it as his own or, if he wished to cancel the engagement, he could ask for the refund of any gifts and payments he had made to her or her family. One of the wives in his compound was appointed as a new intermediary and became the personal "senior wife" of his fiancée. She carried the subsequent installments of bridewealth to the fiancée's house, as well as any other gifts the man wished to make to her or her parents; she also carried messages back and forth, and often gave presents of her own to the fiancée. If they become friendly, the "senior wife" visited the fiancée often, and invited her along if she were going anywhere.

The suitor was expected to visit the girl's parents regularly every twenty-fourth day counting from the day on which they consulted the diviner. He was given food and he often gave the parents a small gift of money for their daughter. Each time he also left a half-penny in cowries under the mat on which he had been sitting. If he and the girl's parents became friendly he visited them frequently, perhaps even every other day. While he was present the girl hid in another room until he left. If she passed his house she shielded her eyes with her hands, and if they met on the street she did not answer his greeting. She was also ashamed to talk to any of the wives of his house except for her personal "senior wife."

Each year during the betrothal, the suitor had to send a total of twenty-four yams to his fiancée's mother during four of the religious festivals; they were pounded into yam loaves, and half were returned with meat stew to the suitor on the following day. The suitor was also expected to send the girl's father an annual gift of one log of firewood from the ita tree; and if he wished, he sent firewood of any kind to him during the cold periods in the dry season and the heavy rains. If the girl's father took a title he had to send a gift known as "title money," which amounted to two shillings six pence, when the cash given as bridewealth totalled five shillings; the value of this gift has also increased markedly. Negligence in any of the obligations to the fiancée's family could lead to arguments, and even to the breaking of the engagement.

During the engagement and continuing as long as the marriage lasted, the suitor had to perform "free labor" when called upon by his father-in-law to do so, usually about once or twice a year; but if the father-in-law were wealthy or had many followers he might never bother to ask for his son-in-law's assistance. This work involved clearing the farm, hoeing yam heaps, building the walls of a house, roofing the house, or providing the rafters and thatch. The man was notified several days in advance so that he could call upon his friends, his relatives, or the members of his club, depending upon the size of the task, to form a working bee (ọwẹ). The father-in-law might give the group something to eat once or twice during the day, but the son-in-law was responsible for food and drink for the feast at the end of the day's work. Building the walls of a house required several days, because each layer of mud was allowed to dry before the next was laid, and the son-in-law usually returned with a different group of men each day, and with female relatives or his wives and members of their clubs to carry water and cook the feast. For roofing, each man brought a bundle of thatch from the farm and provided some of the rafters. As noted earlier the working bee has been dying out; by 1937, it was no longer obligatory after marriage. Ilesha informants say that men are less frequently called upon now for free labor because the bridewealth has risen so high.

After the second installment of bridewealth, the suitor had to contribute two shillings six pence, or less if he could not afford so much, at the death of his fiancée's elder siblings, her parents and their siblings, and her grandparents, and to attend their funerals and those of more distant relatives. This gift, known as "corpse money," has also increased in value, amounting to five shillings for an elder sibling, two pounds ten shillings for a parent, and five pounds for a grandparent. This obligation also continues after marriage.

When the girl reached marriageable age her family notified her suitor that it was time for her to have her body decorated with scarified designs, and he sent six calabashes of water, six bundles of firewood, and the necessary leaves, oils, and other materials. If she had not received them earlier, she was given her facial marks and was excised at the same time, all three operations being performed by a specialist from the compound of "Chief makes beauty" (Owa-ṣe-ẹwa). Palm oil was rubbed into the cuts on the face to prevent them from healing over, and palm kernel oil, charcoal, and a ground leaf (*Eclipta alba* or *Alternanthera nodiflora*) were rubbed into the cuts on the body to give an effect comparable to tatooing. The suitor had to visit his fiancée's house three times daily for four days and on the final day his family sent twelve calabashes of water, twelve bundles of firewood, twelve yams, a large bundle of onions, small calabashes of salt and pepper, two bottles of palm oil, and five shillings six pence. This gift was called "cut money" and was not part of the bridewealth, the second installment of which might be given at the same time. After this the date for the wedding could be set, although it could not be during the same year or before the third installment of the bridewealth was paid.

Weddings were frequently performed in the season after the heavy rains, and were simple, quiet affairs. On the appointed day the families of the bride and groom feasted separately in their respective houses. After dark the bride's "senior wife" and another wife from the groom's house went to her house and brought her back with her possessions after she had been blessed by her father and mother, praying that the marriage would last and be good for her, and that she would become pregnant soon and bear many children. When they returned, the bride was taken to the main chamber where the "senior wife" washed her legs from foot to knee with an infusion of leaves meant to bring her many children. She was then taken to the room of her "senior wife" where she stayed until the groom, who was supposed to be absent, returned; then she was led to his room where she spent the night.

They slept on a mat covered with a white cloth and the bride was expected to prove her virginity. If she did, and informants agree that 90 percent or more did in former times, she was given one shilling six pence as "virginity money" and her husband sent a pot of wine from the oil palm and a pot from the raffia palm, both filled to the brim and covered with leaves, and five yams to her parents. The bloody cloth was carried along for all to see, and there was dancing and rejoicing on the way, joined in by her parents when they arrived. If not, the pots were uncovered and the wine was sloshed around to show that they were only half full, the ends of the yams were cut off, and the cloth was left behind; those who saw these gifts laughed at the bride and made nasty remarks about her. Due largely to greater freedom between young people today, only a small minority of girls are virgins at marriage, and the tests of virginity and the subsequent gifts are usually dispensed with.

Until she had a child, or until they quarreled and separated, the bride lived with her "senior wife," sharing the same room and each other's dishes, clothes, and other property. The bride was instructed to take her "senior wife" as an example, and if she quarreled with her husband, she turned to her for consolation and support. If they liked each other, the bride could run errands for her "senior wife" or help her in selling if she was a trader.

For a period of eighty-four days (three lunar months) the bride made ritual visits to her parents' home, returning to her husband's compound after nightfall. For eight days, starting with the wedding night she spent two nights and two days each in her husband's and in her parents' compounds alternately, returning on the ninth day to make a sacrifice to the God of Divination in her husband's home and remaining in it four nights and days on this occasion. On the thirteenth day she visited her parents but returned to her husband that night and remained there the next three days, and this pattern continued to the eighty-fourth day. On the following day she visited her parents and returned in the afternoon accompanied by many relatives and entered her husband's compound in the daylight, and after this she was free to come and go as she liked.

By 1937 the wedding night had become an occasion for feasting and celebrating throughout the night. The watchnight begins at the bride's house after dark with a feast to which the groom contributes ten yams and ten shillings. It is attended by any of the senior wives from his compound who wish to go, the women of the bride's own compound, usually by the members of the bride's club; if her parents are wealthy, her father's and mother's clubs may also be invited. Following the feast the bride is dressed in her finest clothes, blessed by her father and mother, and accompanied to the groom's house by the entire group. The procession moves slowly through the streets, dancing and singing to the accompaniment of hired drummers. At the groom's compound the bride's legs are washed with the infusion of leaves, and she is led to the room of her "senior wife" where she will live. Her followers stay in the groom's compound until daybreak, singing and making merry.

Two young girls from the bride's clan or from the groom's clan are appointed as "children of the bride" to stay with her in her husband's house to run errands and carry things for her, and to honor her by accompanying her when she goes out. The series of visits of the bride to her parents have not been observed since about 1920; instead the couple remains inside the compound until the fourth day when they both go to visit her parents, accompanied by their club members and wives of the groom's compound. Here there is a second feast, to which the groom contributes the same amount, and in the evening all accompany the couple home. After this, the bride is free to come and go as she wishes.

During the present century, Islamic and Christian marriages have been performed by the mallam, priest, or minister; but by 1937 there had been only about sixty Christian marriages in Ife, plus about sixteen traditional marriages which were subsequently blessed in church. Christian weddings involve a marriage license, a "bachelor's night," a bridal veil, a wedding ring, the throwing of rice, and a wedding cake and dinner. Bridewealth is given in two installments. The first, when the groom is accepted by the bride's family, consists of two pounds ten shillings, forty bitter kola nuts, ten melegueta peppers, a bottle of wine, and a bottle of commercial lemon squash. The second, "love money" consists of ten shillings, a cloth, the engagement ring and wedding cake, a Bible, and contributions to the bride's celebration of the "bachelor's night." Bridewealth is also given in Islamic marriages.

Christian marriage is not popular because by law it must be monogamous. If all previous wives are not relinquished or if subsequent wives are married, the husband can be taken to court and fined. One Ife man tried a church wedding at the time of his sixth marriage; his fifth wife whom he had "inherited" under the levirate had died; his first and third wives had left him; and he left his second and fourth wives so as to have a legal Christian marriage. However his sixth wife committed adultery and, knowing that she could not take him to court, he decided not to try to collect the bridewealth, but married seven other wives, of whom six were still with him in 1937.

Polygyny

Girls are generally married at about twenty, whereas a man does not take his first wife until later unless his father is very wealthy. The age difference between a man and his first wife is usually about ten to fifteen years, and probably was greater in earlier times; and, as men usually take additional wives later in life, this differential increases in subsequent marriages. The significance of this age differential is that between the ages of twenty and thirty-five, women are eligible for marriage while men are not, largely because of the difficulty of accumulating the money for bridewealth. Thus there are "surplus" women who become the plural wives of older men, and it is possible for polygyny to exist even if the numbers of men and women are equal in the population. The effect of this is increased by mortality rates which give a triangular shape to the sex and age distribution of any population so that there are more females in the age bracket of twenty to thirty-five than there are males in the bracket of thirty-five to fifty.

The prevalence of polygyny is shown in the following two tables giving percentages of the heads of 776 families or households in specified categories, based on a survey[9] made in 1951–1953:

TABLE 1

	Abẹokuta	Ijẹbu	Ibadan	Ifẹ	Ilesha	Ondo	All Areas
Wifeless	0.6	—	3.5	2.4	3.7	3.3	2.5
Monogamous	48.7	24.0	38.0	24.1	35.0	30.9	34.9
Polygynous	50.7	76.0	58.5	73.5	61.3	65.8	62.6

TABLE 2

	Abẹokuta	Ijẹbu	Ibadan	Ifẹ	Ilesha	Ondo	All Areas
Wifeless	0.6	—	3.5	2.4	3.7	3.3	2.5
1 wife	48.7	24.0	38.0	24.1	35.0	30.9	34.9
2 wives	30.7	38.0	30.5	32.5	35.0	33.3	32.4
3 wives	17.5	16.0	12.5	24.7	16.3	15.0	17.1
4 or more	2.5	22.0	15.5	16.3	10.0	17.5	13.1

In considering these figures it should be borne in mind that they represent a particular point in time, and that many of the men with only one wife will take additional wives in marriage in later years. Most marriages are polygynous, and

---

[9] Galletti, Baldwin, and Dina 1956:72–73, Tables 25–26.

very few men or women go through life without marrying. Most of the heads of households who had no wives at the time of the survey either had been or would be married. The proportion of household heads with three or more wives was highest in Ifẹ and Ijẹbu and lowest in Abẹokuta, where Christian missions first began their work.

Plural wives give a man prestige because they are an indication of wealth, and they insure him a larger number of children. Polygyny is also satisfying from the woman's point of view, because household duties are shared between co-wives and because a woman's social status is dependent upon that of her husband. A single wife may nag her husband to take an additional wife, and a wealthy woman sometimes provides the bridewealth so that he can do so. However, this too is showing signs of change. In more recent years an increasing number of educated women are arguing that monogamy is preferable to polygyny, and educated men have begun to worry about the cost of supporting more than one wife and, since 1948, the cost of sending their children to university.

A wedding preceded by betrothal is one of three forms of marriage. A woman can also leave her husband for another man, who then becomes responsible for refunding the bridewealth and other wedding gifts to the husband when he sues for divorce, and by doing so he becomes her new husband. Divorce was far less common in the past than it is today. Thirdly, when a man dies his widows become the wives of his younger brothers, a custom known as the levirate and sometimes spoken of as "inheriting" wives. A son can also take a widow of his father, but, of course, not his own mother, as his wife. The affinal bonds established between clans through marriage thus are not terminated by the death of the husband, as his heirs are responsible for the welfare of his widows; yet a woman can, if she desires, return to her own family or take a new husband if the bridewealth is refunded. Neither of these last two forms of marriage involves a wedding. Women have only one wedding, but men may have many if they marry plural wives to whom they have been betrothed.

A husband is expected to provide a room for his wife to live in, to give her money to start her craft or begin trading, and to see that she does not go without food or clothing. Although women expect their husbands to give them gifts, most earn enough to buy their own clothing and some of their own food. Many women are economically independent, and some are wealthier than their husbands. The increasing economic independence of women is sometimes blamed for the increasing frequency of divorce, and it is clearly a contributing factor. Although they may have a favorite wife, men consider it prudent to be scrupulously impartial in giving gifts to their wives.

Death and Burial

If a child dies, no funeral rites are performed; it is considered to be an abiku, one born to die (a-bi-ku), and it is buried immediately in the back yard or the forest without being bathed, shaved, or dressed. In earlier times all childless persons were treated in this fashion; but since about 1920 it has been common custom in Ife to bury childless persons of twenty years and over in the house and to perform a funeral or give a feast for them and for others who are still younger. However, as in the case of all funeral ceremonies, these can be attended only by those who are younger than the deceased.

Christians are buried in the cemetery or on the verandah at the front of their house; depending on their sect, Muslims are buried on the verandah or at a cross-road; but aside from them, the childless, and those who die under special circumstances, all adults are normally buried in the mud floor of the compound to which they belong. Lepers, albinos, hunchbacks, women who die in pregnancy, persons killed by lightning, and others who meet death in special ways are buried in sacred groves of specific deities whose priests make atonements to prevent a recurrence of the misfortune.

A son may beg for permission from his mother's clan to bury her in his compound, and permission to do so is being granted with increasing frequency; but usually her body is covered with a cloth and carried back to her father's compound, where she was born. In cases of matrilocal residence, when a man dies in his wife's compound, his body is carried back to the compound of his birth. However, and this emphasizes the unusual nature of matrilocal residence, it must not be carried out the door; it is taken out through the window in recent times, and, before windows became common, through a hole broken through the wall, and an atonement was made when the hole was repaired.

When a person dies on the farm, the body is carried home for burial; but if it is a child it may be buried there. The carriers are preceded by a man holding a live chicken (adie ibode) some of whose feathers are pulled out and left at every fork in the path. This is to mark the trail so that the soul of the deceased can follow them back to town. When they reach the town gate (ibode), the chicken is killed by striking its head against the ground (formerly the gate) and left there.

Burials are performed by the adult men (isogan) of the sub-clan, headed by the Logun; but those who can trace actual relationship to the deceased, including a man's brothers and sons, do not join them in their duties. The men divide themselves into two groups, one digging the grave and the other bathing the corpse. The corpse is taken outside and seated on an inverted mortar, undressed, and bathed using soap, water, and a loofah sponge, and the head is shaved completely. Care is taken not to allow the head to nod at anyone, for fear that this person will die also. Bathing and shaving are postponed until after dark because of the beliefs that another member of the sub-clan will die if a dead person "sees" its own shadow, and that the man using the sponge will die if he sees the corpse's shadow. The corpse is then dressed again in fine clothes, but all the garments are put on backward so that the soul will know its way back to earth when the time comes for it to be reborn. The waist cloth, worn at the time of death, is inherited by the deceased's youngest child of the same sex; but it and the mortar must be left outside for seven days before they can be used again. A man must never eat food prepared in the mortar on which the body of his wife was washed, and in some compounds an old mortar is kept especially for burials. The sponge and water are thrown away.

The body is then brought into the house and laid on several fine cloths placed on a bed or on a floor mat in a hallway; the body is covered with a still finer cloth, and a small square cloth is placed over the face. Relatives and friends are notified of the death as soon as possible, and they come to console the immediate family and to pay their respects to the departed. A calabash is placed near the body where they may drop a few pennies; these are kept by the wives of the compound, who take turns sitting beside the body, slowly flapping the top cloth to cool it.

The length of the body is measured with a stick and a simple grave is dug in the room of the deceased or, if he had none of his own, in the room of his father. Before beginning their work the grave diggers demand drinks of his children. If there are many children, they may take several days to complete the work so as to enjoy more food and drink, digging only a foot or so and then stopping to eat and drink. If the deceased was elderly, the grave diggers joke while they work to make his children forget some of their sorrow and laugh a little; but if he was their own age or younger, they do not joke while they work and they do not ask for food and drink. The last bit of dirt removed from the grave is saved to be used when creditors come to claim debts owed by the deceased; unless the debts are common knowledge, the creditors are made to eat a little of the dirt while taking an oath that the debts are legitimate.

Each younger sibling by the same father and the same mother is responsible for providing a cloth for the burial. The family of the father of the deceased jointly contributes one cloth, the brothers and sisters of the mother provide one cloth each; close friends may contribute cloths voluntarily. When a man dies, each of his wives must also provide a cloth in return for the one with which he covered her during their first intercourse; but if she has children, they provide the cloth jointly in her name. When a woman dies, her husband and each of her children are responsible for a cloth in which she will be buried. Sisters and daughters share in these responsibilities, even if in former times they had to be indentured to meet them, until they became engaged, after which their "husbands" assume their responsibilities for them. Grandchildren are not expected to contribute to the funerals of their grandparents, unless their own parents are not alive to do so. The body may be buried in as many as eighty cloths, and even a poor family tries to provide at least four. No cloth with any red in it can be used in burial, so that the deceased will not be reborn as a leper.

Interment was formerly delayed as many as eight days, as long as the children of the deceased could afford to feast the male and female members of the sub-clan who were junior to their parent, and their guests. Interment now follows as soon as the grave has been dug, often shortly after the corpse has been bathed and shaved. The body is wrapped in the cloths which have been contributed and tied with skeins of cotton thread. Two hundred cowries (six-tenths of a penny) were traditionally put inside the cloths so that the deceased could pay the gatekeeper of heaven; but by 1937, as much as ten shillings was given by wealthy individuals. If there are enough cloths to hold the body upright, it is balanced and allowed to stand for five minutes or more; but this form of ostentation is dangerous because it is believed that, if the body should fall, a member of the sub-clan will follow it to the grave. If the men who bathe the corpse and dig the grave are pleased with the food and drink they have been given, they carry the corpse about the compound in a farewell visit before it is lowered into the grave, and sometimes the empty coffin is first carried about town.

If a wooden coffin is not used, sticks are laid over the body and marked with the blood and feathers of a chicken (adię ireya), which is killed by stepping on its head and pulling off the head, which is placed in the grave. This is done so that others in the sub-clan will not die. A second chicken (adię iranu) is killed by hitting its head against the wall; its head is pulled off in the same fashion and placed against a wall near the grave, and its blood is put in the grave. This is done to break the ties of the deceased with the members of his sub-clan, so that his soul will not return to trouble them. Both chickens are eaten by the adult men who perform the burial; children of the deceased must not taste them. Hens are used in the burial of women, and cocks when men are buried.

The children of the deceased set a night for a watchnight, often after the burial, but sometimes before, when they provide a feast for the male and female members of the sub-clan who are junior to the deceased, and their guests. Senior clan members do not participate; they must not even taste the food, and they spend the night in their rooms grieving or comforting a close relative of the deceased. They do not contribute to the expenses of the funeral or share in the inheritance. The children of the deceased, his younger brothers and sisters, and his sons-in-law invite their club members and their clubs' drummers to join with them in eating, drinking, singing, and dancing through the night.

This night marks the beginning of funeral ceremonies which can be postponed, rarely more than a year, if the children do not have enough money to do it at once; it is performed as soon as possible so that the parent's soul does not return to cause illness or other misfortune. The watchnight is followed by eight to ten days of feasting, singing, and dancing, if the children can afford it, when relatives and friends of the family come to pay their respects. Formerly it continued through the full three months of mourning, but this was shortened because the Ọni and his chiefs felt that people were spending too much money on funerals; many families had gone into debt, and had had to pawn their children.

On the third day, the husbands of the deceased's sisters and father's sisters, and the husbands of his daughters and brothers' daughters come bringing yam loaves, stew, and one portion of cornstarch porridge for the children's final meal with their parent. The cornstarch porridge and a piece of yam loaf are put into the grave, some of the food is eaten by the children, and the rest is eaten by the men who perform the burial. In order of their seniority the children of the deceased take some earth in their left hand and throw it into the grave while praying that he will find a good place to live in in the afterworld; they are followed by the junior siblings of the deceased and any one who is present. A banana stem is stuck into the earth above the corpse's head, so that when the stem rots there will be a hole through which the soul of the deceased may be fed the blood of sacrificial animals or cooked food. The grave is then completely filled by the grave diggers, moistened, stamped with the heels, and plastered smooth with the hands.

This ends a man's funeral, but for a woman there is another ritual known as "tears of morning." In the morning the wives of the compound into which she was married eat together and then bring large calabashes, which they beat as drums, and dance. Later in the day her eldest child provides a sheep which is killed, cooked, and given with other foods to the wives to eat, after which they resume dancing and singing in honor of her children. This ritual is thought of as a woman's last meeting with the women with whom she has lived since marriage.

After the funeral has been completed, if the children still have enough money, they hire drummers and invite their friends and club members to join them in dancing through the streets to thank those who helped them with the funeral, usually receiving palm wine or money in return; but this custom is also disappearing.

Yoruba funerals are simple but expensive ceremonies that bring younger relatives of the deceased together with their friends in a mood that is festive rather than lugubrious. One grieves at the death of a relative who is younger than himself, or joins those who celebrate the death of elder relatives. Because the latter group is enlarged by hundreds of club members, the festive mood predominates. This is related to the idea that one should be happy when a person has had children and has lived to a ripe old age, and to the concept of fate, to be discussed in the next chapter. It is the duty of the children, who inherit from their parents, to perform the funeral; clan members who are senior to the deceased and cannot inherit are excluded from the festivities. Persons who had no children to perform their funerals were formerly buried without ceremony and without taking the precautions so that they would reach heaven and would be reborn again; but they were considered to be abiku, who would be reborn again anyway. Many of the rituals associated with burial are intended to insure that the deceased will be reborn again, to protect members of the sub-clan from following him to the grave, or to prevent his soul from troubling his descendants. The burial rites vary in minor details from clan to clan, and special rituals are performed if the deceased is a Christian, a Muslim, or a member of the Egungun, Oro, Ifa, Shango, or other religious cults.

7

The Spiritual Cycle

Ifa Divination

SINCE IT WOULD BE IMPOSSIBLE to complete a discussion of the spiritual cycle without a digression about the system of divination known as Ifa, it seems wisest to describe it very briefly at the outset. The *babalawo*, as they are known, are both diviners and priests of Ifa, the God of Divination, and although they are distinguished from the "doctors" or "medicine men," they also prepare charms and medicines. A babalawo consults Ifa by manipulating sixteen palm nuts, which form a large handful, and attempting to pick them all up in his right hand. If one nut remains in his left hand, he makes a double mark in wood dust on his divining tray; if two remain, he makes a single mark.

Four such marks made in a vertical column constitute ȯne half of a figure, and each half has sixteen possible forms. Following the ranking recognized in Ifẹ, and reading from left to right rather than from top to bottom, these sixteen forms can be represented here as: 1111, 2222, 2112, 1221, 1222, 2221, 1122, 2211, 1112, 2111, 1121, 1211, 2212, 2122, 1212, 2121. The second half of the figure, marked in a parallel vertical column, has the same sixteen possible forms; and as they may combine with any of the sixteen forms in the first half of the figure, there is a total of 16 × 16 or 256 complete figures in this complex and rigidly defined system of divination.

Alternatively a babalawo can arrive at the same 256 figures more quickly by a single toss of a chain of eight half seed-shells, although this method is considered less reliable. The chain is held in the middle and cast on the ground so that four half seed-shells fall in a line on each side. A seed falling with the concave inner surface upward is equivalent to a single mark, and one falling with the convex outer surface upward is equivalent to a double mark.

Having arrived at the correct figure, the babalawo recites its verses, one of which is selected as relevant to his client's problem, as in the Chinese I Ching. The verse prescribes the sacrifice required to insure a desired blessing or to avert an impending misfortune. Before a babalawo's apprenticeship is ended in Ifẹ, he must have memorized over a thousand Ifa verses, at least four for each of the 256 figures, and he continues to learn new verses from his colleagues throughout his life. A babalawo can also answer "Yes" or "No" questions by making two tosses of the divining chain and observing which has the higher ranking figure. The babalawo are consulted about a wide range of problems by the worshipers of Ifa and the other deities, as well as by Muslims and Christians.

The same 256 figures, but with different names and different orders and apparently without associated verses, are associated with Sikidy divination in Malagasy, with Agbigba divination in Nigeria, and with "sand cutting" as practiced by many Islamic peoples in west and north Africa. Several other methods of divination are employed among the Yoruba, including "sand cutting," Agbigba, and casting cowries or sections of kola nuts, but Ifa is the most highly regarded.

Multiple Souls and Destiny

Each individual is believed to have at least two souls. The most important is the ancestral guardian soul (eleda, iponri) which is associated with his head, his destiny, and with the belief in reincarnation. The second is the breath (emi) which resides in the lungs and chest and has the nostrils to serve it like the two openings in a Yoruba blacksmith's bellows. The breath is the vital force which makes man work and gives him life. There is also a third soul, the shadow (ojiji), which has no function during life but simply follows the living body about.

One can see the shadow, and hear and feel the breath; but no one hears, feels, or sees the ancestral guardian soul while the individual is alive. The shadow is without substance and requires no nourishment; the breath is sustained by the food which the individual himself eats; but the ancestral guardian must occasionally be fed through sacrifices known as "feeding the head" (ibori, ibo ori). At death the multiple souls leave the body and normally they reach heaven, remaining there until the ancestral guardian soul is reincarnated.

An individual is usually reborn into his own clan, so that the guardian soul is often that of a patrilineal ancestor. The personal names "Father Returns" (Babatunde) and "Mother Returns" (Yetunde) are given to children of the same sex as the reincarnated ancestor, but an ancestor may be reborn in a child of a different sex. The identity of the reincarnated ancestor is determined through physical resemblances, similarities in character or behavior, dreams in which the ancestor tells someone in the family that he has returned, or through divination by a babalawo for the newborn child or for its mother during her pregnancy.

Before a child is born—or reborn—the ancestral guardian soul appears before Olorun, the Sky God, to receive a new body, a new breath, and its destiny (iwa) for its new life on earth. Kneeling before Olorun, this soul is given the opportunity to choose its own destiny, and it is believed to be able to make any choice it wishes, although Olorun may refuse if the requests are not made humbly or if they are unreasonable. Destiny involves a fixed day upon which the souls must return to heaven; and it involves the individual's personality, occupation, and his luck.

The day of one's death can never be postponed, but other aspects of one's destiny may be modified by human acts and by superhuman beings and forces. If one has the full support and protection of his ancestral guardian soul, of Ọlọrun, and of the other deities, he will enjoy the destiny promised him and live out his allotted span of life; if not, he may forfeit blessings destined for him or die before his time. Throughout his life one makes sacrifices to his ancestral guardian and to the deities; he has charms or "medicines" prepared to protect and assist him; and when he is in trouble he consults a diviner to determine what should be done to improve his lot.

Soon after a child is born a babalawo is asked to reveal its destiny. The verse for the figure determined on this occasion may predict the occupation in which the child is most likely to be successful, and in some ways is a chart of his future life. The figure may be carved into a piece of calabash shell so that it will not be forgotten; when the child grows up he can ask a babalawo to recite its verses for him..

In Ifẹ, a babalawo on this occasion determines through "Yes" or "No" questions which ancestral guardian soul has been reborn in the child and which praise names (oriki ipọnri) are appropriate to it. All clan members who share the same ancestral soul and ancestral praise names perform the ceremony of "feeding the head" each year on the same day. A person touches a kola nut to his forehead, breaks the nut into its four sections, and casts them on the ground in a simple form of divination to find if the food he has prepared is acceptable. He also touches to his forehead the plate of food prepared for him and, if an animal is killed, a spot of its blood. Dressed in fine clothes, he remains in his room where he is visited by friends and relatives whom he entertains with food. Close relatives who know his ancestral praise names praise him with them and pray that he will have money, children, and a long and happy life. On this day the souls of ancestors who lived the full span of life allotted to them may return to earth and sit with the living, but they cannot be seen unless one's face has been washed with a special medicine.

Each year children sacrifice to their dead parents at their graves on the day that the parents had sacrificed to their own heads while they were alive; and a Bale does the same for the founder of the sub-clan's compound and joins in the sacrifice to the founder of the clan's senior compound. Children do not sacrifice to a grandparent unless they are specifically told to do so by a babalawo, and there are no sacrifices to other ancestors, unless one accepts the deities as such.

In Ifẹ the ancestral praise names, though taken from the ancestor reincarnated in the individual, go back to a far more remote ancestor (ipọnri) who first had them. Within the clan there are only a limited number of sets of ancestral praise names and these are shared by many clan members, all of whom sacrifice to their ancestral guardian souls on the same day. Thus it seems that while the soul of a recent ancestor is reincarnated in a child, it itself is a part of the soul of a more remote ancestor, and this soul is shared with a number of other living clan members. All clan members bearing the same ancestral praise name are descended spiritually through a series of reincarnations from the remote ancestor who first held these names, as well as patrilineally from the founder of the clan. Although related to the clan, these spiritual descent groups differ from it and from its branches, since the ancestral praise names of an individual may differ from those of his siblings, and are always different from those of his parents.

The ancestral guardian soul is associated with the head, to which sacrifices for it are offered, and it is often said to reside in the head. It is sometimes spoken of as the head (ori) and as the "owner of the head" (olori). A lucky person is called "one who has a good head" (olori rere), and an unlucky person is "one who has a bad head" (olori buruku). To call a Yoruba "olori buruku" is apt to lead to a fight, since it is regarded as an insult and a curse against him and his ancestral guardian; the same is true of the remark, innocuous in English, "Don't be foolish."

At the same time the ancestral guardian is said to remain in heaven, doing exactly the same things in heaven that the individual himself is doing on earth, but, except for twins and abiku, always as an adult. Some believe that there are two ancestral guardian souls, one on earth and one in heaven. Others say that one resides in the forehead, which is associated with luck—a part of one's destiny; a second resides in the crown of the head and guards against evil, and a third resides in the occiput facing backwards and guarding against danger from the rear and the past.

As the occiput warns against dangers from the past, so the big toes tell of good and evil that lie ahead. When one stubs his toe he watches to see whether good or evil ensues, so that he will know which is associated with the right or the left toe. Since others do not know which portends good and which portends evil, it is polite to say "Sorry" whenever a companion stubs his toe. Some Yoruba believe that a separate guardian soul resides in the good toe, but it is usually held that there is only one guardian soul which has different manifestations associated with heaven, the different parts of the head, the big toes and, for some Yoruba, the thumbs.

Intelligence (ọpọlọ), like luck, is associated with the head, with destiny, and with the ancestral guardian. A "soft headed person" (olori riro) can learn quickly because the brain is not hard; while a "hard headed person" (olori lile) is slow in mastering a craft and learning other things. In addition to "feeding the head" one may wash the head with herbs as an atonement or "cooling" (etutu); both are attempts to propitiate the ancestral guardian soul so that it will enable one to enjoy the full measure of luck and intelligence allotted to him by Ọlọrun.

A person who would be called cool-headed in English, one who is even tempered and "keeps his cool," is spoken of as "one who has a soft belly" (oninu riro); whereas a hot-headed person, who is quick tempered and easily offended, is called "one who has a hard belly" (oninu lile). The stomach can cause a man to lose his temper and become involved in a fight which will spoil his luck or "spoil his head." Anger and pleasure are also associated with the stomach. The idiom for "I am angry" is "belly annoys (or 'vexes') me" (inu bi mi), and for "I am pleased" is "belly is sweet (for) me" (inu dun mi). "One who has a bad belly" (oninu buburu) is a wicked person who harms others and whom we would call "hard-hearted"; and a kind, warm-hearted person is "one who has a good belly" (oninu rere). These characteristics are part of the destiny assigned by Ọlọrun before one is born.

If a woman has several children in succession who die at childbirth, in infancy, or even when somewhat older, they may not be several different ancestral souls, but one ancestral soul being repeatedly reborn only to return shortly to heaven where it retains its childlike form. It has been granted short spans of life by Ọlọrun because it does not want to remain long on earth, preferring life in heaven or wishing only to travel back and forth between heaven and earth. Such children are known as abiku or "one born to die"; in a society where infant mortality is high, abiku are common.

Parents may have charms made to keep an abiku from leaving them or they may be told by a babalawo to make a sacrifice or to have the child worship a particular deity. In Mẹkọ and Igana the mother may join a cult group which propitiates abiku and have large iron rattles made for the child to wear on its ankles. Sometimes the corpse of a child is marked by shaving a spot on its head or cutting a notch in its ear so as to prove it is an abiku when it is reborn with the same mark. Sometimes a corpse of an abiku is threatened with burning or with the cutting off of a toe or finger to frighten it into staying on earth when it is reborn again.

Twins (ibeji) are not bad like abiku, but they are feared because they are powerful. It is believed that the mother will not conceive again unless they are propitiated properly. It is also believed that if boy twins reach adulthood they will inadvertently cause the death of their father by their power, as female twins can cause the death of their mother. In Ife it was formerly customary for parents to allow the weaker or uglier twin to die of neglect, regardless of its sex, and to bury it in the forest. When twins are born two small pots are partially buried in the corner of a room and sacrifices are offered near these annually. When a twin dies, the parents have a woodcarver fashion a small twin figure (ere ibeji) of the same sex and with the facial marks of its clan. Twins must be treated equally, even if one is dead, and some parents give the figure the same kind of beads, bracelets, and earrings that they give the living one. If the second twin dies while young, another figure is carved and dressed in the same way. Twins and abiku are not deities; sacrifices offered to them are for their souls. Like abiku, twins retain the form of children in heaven, and spend their time at play. Triplets and quadruplets are even more feared than twins, but they are uncommon, whereas judging from the number of Yoruba twin figures in existence, twins are unusually numerous.

The breath can leave the body in dreams, as it leaves the sleeping body of a "witch" (ajẹ) to perpetrate evil. An Ife man who claimed and was credited with a dozen deaths by magic, said that there is a medicine which enables one to see the breath of a living person and to predict his death if, for example, one sees it tied and bound and being dragged away by a practitioner of evil magic or "wizard" (oṣo). Another medicine can be used to trap the breath during dreams, preventing its return to the body and causing the victim to die within four days. Both the breath and the ancestral guardian soul have the form of the individual and can be recognized.

Another charm or medicine is reputed to insure that one will live to reach the day appointed by Ọlọrun for his souls to return to heaven. This day cannot be altered except by suicide, in which case the souls never return to heaven. It cannot be postponed by prayers, sacrifices, magic, or any other means. The allotted span of life can never be extended, but it can be shortened by offended deities, by evil spirits, by swearing falsely, by "witches" and "wizards," by the curses or evil magic of one's enemies, at human hands as punishment for a crime, and in other ways. One who has lived until the day assigned him is spoken of as "one who has (his) day" (olojo); but a child who dies when only a few years or a few days old may also have lived out his allotted span, as in the case of abiku.

The Afterworld

Immediately after death the breath[10] makes farewell visits to clan members who are away from home. It appears, for example, to a relative in Ibadan or Lagos and asks if he has heard word of a death at home. The relative is unaware that his visitor is dead, but he will learn of his death within a day or so. This is the last time the dead speak to living relatives except in dreams. Afterward the presence of a dead person may be felt, as when someone whom you cannot see is standing beside you and you feel a chill, but he cannot speak.

If a person has lived his full span of life, his multiple souls proceed to the afterworld together. Those who die before their time is up remain on earth as ghosts, but they go away to distant towns where they are not known and settle there as traders. They can talk to people who had not known them previously, and to them they seem like normal living persons. They may marry and have children, and one may marry a ghost without knowing it. If someone whom the ghost knew before death comes to town, it disappears. Finally, when the day appointed by Olorun arrives, the ghost "dies" a second death and goes to heaven.

When the three souls reach heaven the ancestral guardian soul gives an account of all the good and bad deeds done on earth, just as a man on earth is heard in court, and Olorun judges his case. If a man has been good and kind on earth his souls are sent to the "good heaven" (orun rere); but if he has been cruel or wicked and guilty of murder or theft, of beating or poisoning others, or of injuring them through bad magic or slander, he is condemned to the "bad heaven" (orun buburu, orun buruku) as punishment. There are two heavens, both located in the same part of the universe, where evil deeds are punished and earthly wrongs are righted. The same word (orun) is used for the sky and for the afterworld, which is generally believed to be near Olorun, the Sky God, in or beyond the sky. However, some say it may be elsewhere as the dead are said to travel there on foot, crossing rivers and climbing mountains, and buying food on the way with the money spent by their relatives at their funerals. The wicked and unkind meet dangerous animals on the road, have to cross rivers swollen in flood, encounter mountains so slippery that they take years to climb, and must spend all their money so that they go hungry on their journey.

In the good heaven or "heaven of breezes" (orun afefe) the air is fresh and

---

[10] In Igana and Oyo it is the shadow that makes these visits and that leaves the body in dreams; but it is the breath in Ife and Meko.

good, and life goes on as it does on earth. The dead carry on their earthly occupations as farmers or drummers, and the poor are still poor and the chiefs are still
chiefs. However, if a title has been held on earth by a candidate who did not deserve
it, it is given to the rightful candidate in heaven. All thefts and losses are restored
to their rightful owners. There is a whole series of men who have held the same
title in succession, and they are seated on a mat in order of their seniority. Before
a dead person can take his place, his funeral must be performed on earth and his
head must be shaved again in heaven. There are towns of the Ifẹ, Ọyọ, Ijẹbu, and
other Yoruba subgroups; of the Igbo, Hausa, and other African peoples; and of the
nations of Europe and America. Clans are reunited in heaven, but there is considerable difference of opinion as to whether a wife lives with her husband or
returns to her father; and some hold that the babalawo live with Ifa, those who die
in battle live with Ogun, the God of Iron and War, and the albinos, hunchbacks,
and dwarfs live in the garden of Orishala, the God of Whiteness, who created
them.

In the bad heaven or "heaven of potsherds" (ọrun apadi) the cruel people
are beaten and made to walk in the midday sun. Although missionaries have attempted to equate it with hell as a place heated with charcoal like a pottery kiln,
it is thought of as hot like pepper, not hot like fire. The symbolism of potsherds
refers to broken pots that can never be put together and used again; the souls of
those who go to the heaven of potsherds can never be restored to the living through
reincarnation.

Suicides, like cruel people, can never be reincarnated. They can never reach
heaven and, having renounced earth, belong to neither. They become evil spirits
and cling to the treetops like bats or butterflies.

While one is alive he tries to be kind to others and he prays that he will
be able to go to the good heaven and return again, and will not die never to return
to earth. It is not that the good heaven is not pleasant, but one wishes to return to
earth in another generation to be with his children and grandchildren.

8

The Deities

Selecting One's Deity

THE YORUBA BELIEVE IN MANY DEITIES (ẹbọra, ẹbura, imọlẹ, orisha), the full number never having been recorded. Some say there are 400 or 401, others that there are 600 or 601, and some even more; but these numbers are only figurative. Some are worshiped throughout Yoruba land and have their counterparts among neighboring peoples; some are fairly widely known; and some are only of local significance. Only some of the more important deities can be discussed here.

Except for Ọlọrun, the deities are believed to have lived on earth, but instead of dying they became gods. The worshipers of a deity are spoken of as his "children," even though the members of a cult may not be related to each other. The worship of the deities completely overshadows the worship of the ancestors, which is so important in most African societies.

An individual normally worships the deity of his father, and some also worship their mother's deity as well. Many deities are identified with a particular clan in which case all members, male and female, are worshipers by virtue of birth into it. After marriage women return home for the annual festival of their own deity, but they assist in the performance of the annual festival of their husband's deity. If a woman is childless, despite prayers and sacrifices to her husband's and her own deity, she may seek the help of another deity. Through divination at her husband's or her own shrine, or by consulting a babalawo, she may be directed to a particular deity, or she may choose one because of its reputation for giving children. If she bears a child within a year, it belongs to the deity who "gave" it to her, and the child is brought up as its worshiper.

Outsiders from other clans can also be brought into many cult groups in another way. A deity may claim a person as a worshiper by driving him into the forest where he wanders about not knowing where he is or what he is doing, by tormenting him in dreams, or by causing him illness or misfortune. In this case it may be necessary to consult a babalawo to determine the identity of the deity who is causing the trouble.

As a child usually worships the deity of his father, so the child of a convert to Christianity or Islam follows his father's religion. And just as a worshiper of Ifa can be converted to Christianity or Islam, so Ifa (and other deities) can claim a convert by "fighting" with him. Agbọnbọn was the son of a babalawo who had been converted to Christianity. Before his father died, while they were at Ishọya during the second evacuation of Ifẹ, he told Agbọnbọn that he had been born to become a babalawo and gave him a divining chain. When Agbọnbọn returned to Ifẹ, his seven wives and all his children suddenly died, and he wrapped up his set of palm nuts and £2 10s. 0d. that he had, and started out of town to die by himself in the forest. A friend whom he met on the way convinced him that he should consult a babalawo. When he did, he was told that Ifa was fighting with him, that he should worship Ifa and become a babalawo. He did so and prospered. In 1937 he was the most respected diviner in Ifẹ, and he had so many wives and children that he said he had lost count of them.

In another instance, a woman at Mẹko told how her mother's father did not return home one night. The next day his children went to a diviner to find out what had happened, and they were told that he had been carried away into the forest by Ọshọsi, a Hunter God. The next day hunters and other people went out to look for him, some going as far as fifteen miles from town, but they could not find him. His children went to the priest of Ọshọsi, who told them that if they did not promise to worship Ọshọsi well, they would never see their father again; but if they promised to do so, and made a sacrifice, they would find him. The priest said that there was no need to go to the far forest, because their father was close to town. They made the promise and offered the sacrifice, and the next day their father was found sitting beside a tree, not far from the road, only about a hundred yards from town. The father himself did not want to be initiated, although his own mother had been, so he gave a daughter to Ọshọsi instead and she was initiated two years later.

Those who are claimed by having a deity "fight" with them are usually initiated into the cult through ceremonies which once lasted several months but have been shortened to a few weeks. They are secluded in the shrine where they are taught the rituals of worship, and finally their head is shaved and the deity possesses them.

When possession occurs it is believed that the deity mounts the initiate, entering his head and taking control of his body. The person is spoken of as the "horse" or the "mount" of the deity, who may speak through him, asking for sacrifices and predicting good or bad fortune. Some deities, like Ifa and Odua, never possess. Shango possesses each initiate after his head has been shaved, but at his annual festivals only one individual in a given cult group is possessed. Other deities, like Yemọja and Ọshun, can possess dozens of worshipers at the same time during their annual festivals.

Ọlọrun, the Sky God

Ọlọrun, who is also known as Olodumare, is the Sky God and has been syncretized with the Christian God and the Muslim Allah. He created (or is the father of) all other deities, and, like Nyame among the Ashanti and other West African "high gods," he stands above and beyond them. Unlike other deities he has no special worshipers or cult; prayers are addressed to him, but no sacrifices are offered directly to him, and he has no shrines. Nevertheless he is neither so remote nor unconcerned that he does not intervene in affairs on earth, and most of the sacrifices prescribed by the babalawo are taken to Olorun by Eshu, after having been placed at one of Eshu's many shrines. As the deity who assigns and controls the individual destinies of mankind, Olorun can be considered as the God of Destiny.

Eshu, the Divine Messenger

Eshu, also known as Elegba or Elegbara, is the youngest and cleverest of the deities. He is the divine messenger who delivers sacrifices prescribed by the babalawo to Olorun after they have been placed at his shrine, a simple chunk of laterite set outside of every Ife compound or a crude mud figure as in Meko. He is a trickster who delights in trouble making, but he serves Olorun and the other deities by causing trouble for human beings who offend or neglect them. Even Shango, a God of Thunder, who can kill a person with lightning, must first ask Eshu to "open the road" for him; or he may ask Eshu to use the variety of punishments at his command. Eshu is notorious for starting fights, killing people in traffic and hunting accidents, or by toppling walls and trees on them, and he causes calamities to the deities and humans alike. Humans may also send Eshu to fight with their enemies by naming them while putting palm kernel oil on the laterite that serves as his shrine, and then mentioning their own name while adding palm oil as an atonement so that Eshu will not turn against them for having violated his taboo.

Eshu is also the divine enforcer, punishing those who fail to make the sacrifices prescribed by the babalawo and rewarding those who do. When any of the deities wishes to do good for those on earth, he sends Eshu to do it for him. His role as the messenger who delivers sacrifices to Olorun and does good deeds on behalf of the other deities, and his remarkable even-handedness in his role as the divine enforcer are hardly consistent with his identification as Satan by Christians and Muslims, which can only be understood as the result of a failure to find the equivalent of the Devil in Yoruba belief.

Regardless of what deity they worship, everyone prays frequently to Eshu so that he will not trouble them; and everyone sacrifices to him since a bit of every sacrifice to Olorun and to other deities is set aside for him. In addition, he has his own worshipers and priests, who are identified by a string of small opaque maroon or black beads worn around the neck. Palm kernel oil, which is used to make Eshu fight, is his strongest taboo, and his worshipers must not eat it, rub their bodies with it, or have it near them; and no one can whistle at his shrine. His favorite foods, which are offered to him as sacrifices, are palm oil, boiled corn and beans, male animals and fowl, palm wine and other kinds of liquor, and many other foods.

Ifa, the God of Divination

Ifa, also known as Ọrunmila and Agbọnniregun, is the God of Divination and a close friend of Eshu. He is often spoken of as a scribe or clerk because he "wrote" for the other deities and he taught the babalawo to "write" the figures of Ifa on their divining trays. He is also described as a learned man or scholar because of all the knowledge and wisdom in the Ifa verses, and as the interpreter between the gods and humans. Ọlọrun gave him the power to speak for the gods and communicate with human beings through divination. When the God of Thunder or the God of Whiteness or any other deity wishes a special sacrifice, he can send a message to the human beings on earth through Ifa.

Most importantly Ifa is the one who transmits and interprets the wishes of Ọlọrun to mankind, and who prescribes the sacrifices which Eshu carries to him. The importance of Ifa divination, as compared to simpler methods using cowries and kola nuts, is probably due to the fact that, except for prayers, it provides the most direct access to Ọlọrun, who controls men's destinies. Whatever personal deities they may worship, all believers in the Yoruba religion turn to Ifa in time of trouble, and on the advice of the babalawo all sacrifice to Eshu and through him to Ọlọrun. This important trinity is public and available to all, and together Ọlọrun, Ifa, and Eshu grant and assist humans to achieve the destinies which are assigned each individual before his ancestral guardian soul is reborn.

Not all worshipers of Ifa become babalawo, which involves not only a very expensive initiation, but also years of apprenticeship to learn the figures and the verses with their associated sacrifices and medicines. The babalawo use plates, elaborately carved wooden "cups," or wooden bowls in which to store their sixteen palm nuts; divining trays on which the Ifa figures are marked in wood dust; divining "bells" or tappers with which the tray is tapped to call Ifa's attention before beginning to divine; and bags in which they carry their divining chains and other materials. They are distinguished by a string of alternating opaque tan and light green beads worn on the left wrist, although some also wear solidly beaded bracelets of many different colors. They serve as priests for the other Ifa worshipers, divining for them at the annual festival after having offered a sacrifice to Ifa's sacred palm nuts. Ifa's favorite foods include she-goats, dried rats, dried fish, snails, and kola nuts. His taboos include a kind of duiker (etu), a kind of monkey (ẹdun), and a kind of rat (okete), none of which can be eaten by a babalawo.

Odua, the Creator of the Earth and His Allies

Odua, also known as Odudua or Oduduwa, is the Creator of the Earth, as recounted in Chapter 1. He is considered the progenitor of all the Yoruba, and the first to rule on earth as King of Ife. He is the most important deity in Ife because of his association with the Ọni who, like the other Yoruba kings, validates his status and authority by claiming direct descent from Odua in the male line.

Odua and the deities who sided with him in his fight with Orishala do not possess their worshipers; their worshipers wear no beads, drink wine from the oil palm but observe a taboo on wine from the raffia palm, and beat iron rods instead of drums.

One of those who supported Odua was Ọbameri, whose priests must be called to supervise the burial of people who hang themselves and to make an expensive atonement so that this misfortune will not happen again in the clan; sacrifices are brought to him annually by the traders who sell sheep and goats so that he will not cause them to hang themselves with the ropes with which they tether their animals in the market. Another ally was Ẹshidalẹ, whose priests make atonement for and supervise the burial of those who commit suicide by jumping up from the ground and landing on their heads. Others were Ẹlẹshijẹ, the God of Medicine, who is the owner of herbs and the patron of the doctors; and Ọrẹ, a God of the Hunt, by whom oaths are sworn in cases of theft and whose priests make atonement for those guilty of incest. Ẹlẹshijẹ and Ọrẹ are the Ife counterparts of Ọsanyin and Ọshọsi in other Yoruba areas, but Ọbameri and Ẹshidalẹ are little known outside of Ifẹ.

Orishala, the God of Whiteness and His Allies

Orishala or Oshala is best described as the God of Whiteness because the color white is especially appropriate to him and because his name means "God of the White Cloth" (Orisha ala); but he is also the Creator of Mankind, having made the first man and woman, and his role is that of fashioning the form of human beings in the womb before they are born. Working in the darkness with a knife, he shapes their bodies like a woodcarver, and then separates the arms, legs, fingers, and toes, and opens the eyes, ears, nose, and mouth.[11] He is sometimes called Ọlọrun's sculptor. Those that he fashions as albinos (afin), hunchbacks (abuke), cripples (arọ), dwarfs (arara), and dumb mutes (odi) are sacred to Orishala. They are not the result of his mistakes; he makes them this way to mark them as his worshipers so that his worship will not be forgotten. Children born in a caul or with the umbilical cord wrapped around the neck are also sacred to him, and among the names given to them are some referring to the "white cloth" (ala) in which they were born.

Orishala is also known as "King of the White Cloth" (Ọbatala). His worshipers may wear cloths of other colors, but white cloths are considered proper. Women worshipers wear as necklaces strings of small opaque white beads and often white lead anklets and bracelets; some have ivory bracelets and lead staffs and fans. The symbol to which his sacrifices are offered is one or more flattish sections of bone or ivory. Live snails are often kept in his shrines to be offered in sacrifice and some of the many other foods sacrificed to him are also white: boiled

---

[11] According to his worshipers, Ọbameri as owner of the head makes the head before Orishala fashions the body; and according to the worshipers of Ogun, the God of Iron, it is Ogun who does the knife work after Orishala has modeled the body.

corn, shea butter, melon-seed oil, yams, cornstarch gruel, and coconuts. Foods cooked for him should not be seasoned with salt, pepper, or palm oil. Many of his worshipers cook with shea butter or melon-seed oil instead of the orange-red palm oil, and use shea butter in place of palm oil in their lamps. Orishala's principal taboos are wine from the oil palm, as explained in the creation myth, and dogs. He fights with those who offend him by causing their stomachs to swell, and it is believed that if a dog should enter his shrine it will die. Fire should not be kindled in his shrine, the outer walls of which are decorated with white designs made with chalk.

Orishala is also known as the "Big Orisha" (Orishanla), referring to the fact that he is the most important of the "white deities" (orisha funfun) of whom there are over fifty. Like the followers of Odua, the white orishas form a major subdivision in the Yoruba pantheon; the word "orisha," which is sometimes used for the deities in general, has a more specific reference to the members of this group, for whom wine from the oil palm is also taboo. Among those who supported Orishala in his fight with Odua were Orisha Alashe, or Oluorogbo, who is said to have owned the loop-handled quartz stools found at Ife and to have saved the world by bringing rain at a time of great drought and famine; Orisha Ikire, a warrior who had great wealth and many slaves and who can cause dumb mutes to be born to those who neglect him; and Orisha Teko or Orisha Ijugbe, the Ife counterpart of Orisha Oko, God of the Farm. With some exceptions, such as flagellation by the worshipers of Orisha Ogiriyan or Orisha Ogiyan, the worship of the white deities is so similar that in specific cases it becomes difficult to say whether one is speaking of separate deities or simply of separate names or manifestations of Orishala. Functions ascribed to one of them in one town may be ascribed to another elsewhere. The priests of Orishala, or of one of the other white deities, must be called to perform the burial and atonement when a woman dies in pregnancy. Under the cover of darkness, and with great secrecy, they carry the body to the sacred grove of Orishala where it is cut open and the fetus is removed and buried in a separate grave.

Ogun, the God of Iron

Ogun, who supported Odua in his fight with Orishala, is the God of Iron and the patron of all those who use iron tools. He is a patron of hunters and warriors and thus a God of War, a patron of blacksmiths, of woodcarvers and leatherworkers, of barbers, of those who perform circumcision and cicitrization, and in recent times a patron of locomotive and automobile drivers. For this reason it is said that there are seven kinds of Ogun, one being the patron of worshipers who wear snakes around their bodies; but there are more than seven classes of people who are indebted to him because they use iron implements. Without him people could not have their hair cut, they could not be circumcised or have facial marks, animals could not be hunted or butchered, farms could not be cleared or hoed, paths to the farms and water holes would be overgrown with weeds, and no one could have made fire without the strike-a-lights which were used before matches were imported. The other deities are also dependent on Ogun, because he clears the path for them with his machete; but he is most renowned as a blacksmith and a great warrior. Ogun is the principal deity of the city of Ilesha, for which he stands as Odua does for Ife.

Ogun is the owner of iron and of palm fronds which are used to mark his shrines; they may be used by other deities, but they belong to him. He is also the owner of dogs; his worshipers eat dogs and male dogs are one of his favorite sacrificial foods. Other foods include he-goats, cocks, tortoises, snails, maize beer, palm wine, and boiled corn and beans. A machete, a gun, or any piece of iron may be used as his symbol when offering sacrifices to him or when swearing oaths by him. A large piece of iron, shaped like a tear drop and weighing over a hundred pounds, is kept in the Oni's palace for swearing by Ogun in cases heard by the Ife chiefs.

Among Ogun's taboos are crickets and an unidentified venomous snake (perhaps cobra or viper); but these apply to blacksmiths and not to all classes of Ogun worshipers. The smithy serves as a refuge for anyone who is losing a fight, and whistling in the smithy is taboo. With Eshu's help Ogun fights with those who offend him or swear falsely in his name by causing them to be bitten by a snake, shot by a hunter, injured in a traffic accident, cut with a knife, or stuck with a needle; or a hunter may step on a pointed stick or his gun may explode, and a blacksmith may pound his finger. If Ogun is fighting with a person, any of these accidents can cause his death. As insignia, the Ogun worshipers may wear palm leaves tied around the wrist, or iron necklaces, or several iron bracelets.

Oranmiyan, the Son of Ogun and Odua

Oranmiyan or Oranyan is said to have had two fathers, Ogun and Odua. A myth tells how Ogun brought back many slaves from a battle and gave them all to Odua, the king, except a woman named Lakange with whom he had fallen in love. When Odua learned that he had kept Lakange for himself, he commanded Ogun to bring her to him. Ogun did so, but he explained that he had already had intercourse with her. Nevertheless Odua took her as his wife, and when she gave birth to Oranmiyan, he was half white skinned like Odua and half black skinned like Ogun. In commemoration of this in Ife, young Emese run through the streets with the right half of their bodies colored red[12] with camwood and the left side colored white with chalk during the Olojo festival in honor of Ogun and Oranmiyan.

Oranmiyan became a great warrior like his father, Ogun. He became the founder and the first king of Oyo, and he ruled as king of Ife after his father, Odua. Except for the Owa of Ilesha, Yoruba kings formerly sent to Eredumi, the chief priest of Oranmiyan at Ife, for his sword of state and it is said that the king of Benin and the kings of the Egun, Fon, and Gan did so also. This sword sym-

---

[12] Akogun, the town chief responsible for the worship of Oranmiyan, said that camwood is used because no one would wish to be colored black with charcoal. Eredumi, his priest, said that Oranmiyan was half red and half white.

bolizes the right to execute criminals and thus the right to rule as king.

A tall granite monolith at Ifẹ is said to be the staff which Ọranmiyan carried to war, and a large stone slab is his shield; but his sacrifices are offered at the spot where he is said to have gone into the ground when he became a deity. His favorite sacrificial animal is a ram, and his taboos include wine from the raffia palm, chicken cooked with melon seed oil, and two stew leaves. His worshipers wear no beads or other insignia but Eredumi, his chief priest, carries a wooden staff topped by a human figure.

Shango, the God of Thunder and His Counterparts

Shango is the Ọyọ God of Thunder and a son of Ọranmiyan. Living in the sky he hurls thunderstones to earth, killing those who offend him or setting their houses afire. His thunderbolts (ẹdun ara) are prehistoric stone celts which farmers sometimes find while hoeing their fields; they are taken to Shango's priests who keep them at his shrines as the symbols through which Shango is fed. When a house is struck by lightning his priests, who are distinguished by the appliquéd leather shoulder bags (laba) that they carry, are called to remove the thunderstone from the ground. Until they have performed an atonement to prevent a recurrence, a house struck by lightning must not be rebuilt—its inhabitants sleeping in the interim in smithies and market stalls—and a person killed by lightning must not be buried.

Shango fights with troublemakers and those who use bad medicine to harm others, as well as with his worshipers who offend him in other ways. His taboos include the Redflanked Duiker, a rat (ago), and sese beans. One must not carry fire or smoke in front of a person who is possessed by Shango. His favorite foods include rams, bitter kola nuts, yam porridge, bean stew, and ochra stew. His worshipers wear a string of alternating small red and opaque white beads as their insignia.

The one member of the cult group who is possessed at Shango's festival is known as his "mount" (Ẹlegun). He is the only cult member who actually dances with the carved wooden wands (oshe Shango) which every initiate receives for his personal shrine. He wears a cotton coat to which are fastened charms or miniature combs, dance wands, and thunderstones carved in wood, and which may be blackened with the blood of many sacrifices. He also wears appliquéd cotton panels (wabi) about his waist which whirl out from his body as he dances, knee-length cotton trousers colored red with camwood and trimmed with cowries, and, on occasion, a large red cape.

As the son of Ọranmiyan, Shango is said to have succeeded his father as one of the early Alafin or kings of Ọyọ. He was feared because when he spoke fire came out of his mouth, and he was noted for his magical powers. His mount performs magical tricks to impress the spectators, such as sitting on an iron spear point, releasing people tied with ropes, and passing an iron rod through his tongue. He and his assistants carry long blackened staffs which make a mysterious rustling

A shrine for Shango, God of Thunder, at Mẹkọ, 1950. In the center is the inverted mortar (odo Shango), decorated with a human face and a ram's head, which serves as a stool when initiates are shaved. On it sits a plate with horns and "thunderstones" inside, and leaning against it, behind two horns, is a gourd rattle (shẹrẹ Shango). A second inverted mortar is at the far left. Three dance wands (oshe Shango) lean against the wall, on which are hung four appliquéd leather shoulder bags (laba Shango).

sound, and in states of possession he may carry a pot of live coals on his head, put his hand into the pot, or eat fire without apparent harm. According to a myth it was a defeat in a magical contest that led Shango to leave Ọyọ and hang himself, although when lightning flashes his worshipers shout "The king did not hang himself" (Ọba ko so).

Shango and the deities associated with him are for the people of Ọyọ what Odua and his followers are for the people of Ifẹ. Shango's counterpart in Ifẹ is Ọramfẹ, whose priests make atonement when lightning strikes; but they do not save the thunderstones he throws and they do not use the gourd rattles, appliquéd bags, or dance wands of Shango. His priests bury hunchbacks and cripples and make atonements for them. In the Ketu kingdom to the west there is a third God of Thunder, Agbona, with yet a different set of paraphernalia.

River Gods and Goddesses

Ọya is the Goddess of the Niger River and the favorite wife of Shango. Shango had other river goddesses as wives, but only Ọya remained true to him until the end, leaving Ọyọ with him and becoming a deity when he did. Ọya manifests herself as the strong wind which precedes a thunderstorm. When Shango wishes to fight with lightning, he sends his wife ahead of him to fight with wind. Without her, Shango cannot fight, and when Ọya comes, people know that he is not far behind. Ọya blows roofs off houses, knocks down large trees, and fans the fire set by Shango's thunderbolts into a high blaze.

Ọya fights with her own worshipers who have offended or neglected her by afflicting them with a throat disease which may be fatal. Her principal taboos are rams and ewes, and no one may smoke or have a fire in her shrine or in front

(a) A "mount" of Shango, the God of Thunder, dancing at Ọyọ, 1951. His hair is braided like a woman's. His shirt is cotton colored red with camwood and covered with cowry shells; charms are fastened in front. Below the shirt are appliquéd panels (wabi) of cloth which fly out when he whirls and turns. Behind him a man holds one of the staffs which make a rustling sound, and the boy at the right carries the type of drum (bata) which is appropriate for Shango. The dog, sacred to Shango, is dressed in appliquéd cloths; it can eat freely in the market without fear of being beaten.

(b) Worshippers of Ẹrinlẹ, a Hunter God, carrying his shrine figures to the river at his annual festival at Igana, 1951. The hunter's leather fly whisk with the wooden handle carved as a human figure, worn on the shoulder of the man at the left, is one of Ẹrinlẹ's insignia, as is the iron bracelet on his wrist.

(c) A diviner (babalawo) marking a figure of Ifa divination in wood dust on his Ifa tray. He holds the sixteen palm nuts which are manipulated to determine the figure, and, in front of the tray, is a seventeenth palm nut set on a ring of cowry shells. At the left, beside the tray, is the diviner's cow tail fly whisk, and at the right is the bowl in which the palm nuts are stored. Ifẹ, 1937.

of a worshiper in a state of possession. Her favorite sacrificial foods include she-goats, castrated he-goats, hens, plantains, brown beans, and mashed corn. Oya's symbols are polished stone celts which are obtained from the Shango worshipers; they resemble Shango's thunderstones, but their cutting edges are not as sharp. Horns of the African buffalo ("bush-cow") are also kept at her shrines, and as insignia her worshipers wear strings of tubular maroon beads around the neck.

Yemoja is the Goddess of the Ogun River, which flows southward past the cities of Oyo and Abeokuta. Some say her work was selling meat; others say that she dyed cloth and shelled melon seeds. She came from near Bida, in Nupe territory, to old Oyo where she married the king, Oranmiyan, and by him bore Shango. Later she left Oranmiyan and married Okere, chief of the town of Shaki; but Okere made insulting remarks about her long breasts and when she fled with her pots, he knocked her down and she turned into the Ogun River. The versions of this myth differ, but it is cited as the reason why the successors to the title of Okere must cover their face when they cross the Ogun River on their way to Oyo.

Yemoja's main symbols are small river-worn stones through which sacrifices are offered to her, and, secondarily, a set of sixteen cowry shells which her worshipers use in divination. Her shrine also contains a pot from which water is given to newborn children and to women who come to beg Yemoja for children. During her annual festival carved wooden figures which decorate her shrines and bowls to bring back fresh water for the shrine are carried on the head to a nearby river. The women who carry the bowls of water are possessed by Yemoja on their way back to the shrine, but they must not speak or spill a drop of water as they dance through town.

Yemoja's insignia is a string of small glass beads, crystal clear "like water," which is worn around the neck. Her favorite foods are mashed corn, yam loaf, yam porridge, goats, hens, ducks, and fish. Her main taboos are dogs, ochra leaves, and two other stew leaves; it is believed that any dog who eats any part of a sacrifice to Yemoja will die. Many Yemoja worshipers also observe the taboos of her son, Shango. Yemoja fights with those who offend her by causing a stomach ache, or by carrying them away in a river. However, the atonement for those who die by drowning is made by the priests of another deity, Erinle.

Erinle (Eyinle, Enle) was a hunter who is the deity of a small river near Ilobu. He was trying to seduce Oba, a River Goddess who was a wife of Shango, and Shango fought him with magic. Shango's magic was stronger, and in annoyance Erinle threw himself down on the ground and water burst out of the spot. River-worn stones are his symbol; they are kept at his shrine along with a pot of water, raphia which Erinle is said to own, and a forged iron standard decorated with an iron bird, somewhat like that which is used for his associate, Osanyin. As in the case of Yemoja, his worshipers carry carved wooden shrine figures on their heads when they go to a nearby river to get water during his annual festival, at which time possession occurs. He also fights by drowning those who offend him and his priests bury the body at the river near where it is found; they also take all of the deceased's personal property and make an atonement so that another member of his clan will not be drowned. Erinle's principal taboo is elephant meat, and his sacrificial foods include dogs, he-goats, cocks, pigeons, white steamed beans, and

(a) *An Egungun of the alagọ category at Igana, 1938. Note the absence of a carved mask.*

(b) *"Children of Egungun" dancing at Igana, 1938. The appliquéd panels of the costume fly out as the dancers whirl about. Again there are no carved masks. Note the netting through which the dancer on the left sees out, and the roofs thatched with grass.*

yam loaf. His worshipers are distinguished by an iron chain with distinctive links worn on the right wrist as a bracelet, and a hunter's fly whisk worn on the shoulder.

There are a number of other river gods and goddesses (Ọba, Yewa, Ondo, and Arẹ), of whom the most important is Ọshun. The Ọshun River rises in Ekiti in the east and flows past the city of Oshogbo where her principal shrine, attended by a virgin and decorated with figures cast in brass, is located. Her principal symbols are river-worn stones, and small brass rods which distinguish her from other river deities. Her shrines also include pots of water from which her worshipers may drink, and sixteen cowries which they use in divination.

Ọshun is the owner of brass, and her worshipers wear brass bracelets as their insignia and dance holding a brass fan or a brass sword. She fights by causing dysentery, stomach ache, and menopause. Her principal taboos are guinea corn, guinea corn beer, and snails. Her foods include a thin soup made of wild lettuce, yam porridge, bean porridge, several other bean dishes, and honey. Her favorite drink is maize beer.

Ọshun is the Yoruba Venus, renowned for her beauty and for her meticulous care of her appearance. Tall, light skinned, and with beautiful breasts, she is described as bathing several times a day, primping before a mirror, and wearing brass bracelets from the wrist to the elbow. Her hair was long and straight until Yemọja, who is black-skinned, stole it from her while Ọshun was busy at her indigo dye-pots. Ọshun cast her sixteen cowries and learned that Yemọja was the thief, but she was unable to recover her hair. So she added grass, cloth, and indigo dye to what little hair she had left and made a top-knot, which is like the false hairpiece worn by her priests at Oshogbo.

Because of her great beauty, Ọshun was desired by all the gods, and she took many of them as husbands or lovers. Her amorous adventures complicate the divine genealogies, but her worshipers take pride in these adventures because they add to her reputation for beauty and desirability. They even describe her as a harlot, and one, with obvious amusement, said that she was a "civilized woman," like the modern Nigerian school girls.

Accounts vary, but it is said that she married Ogun, and Shango fought with him and took her away. She left Shango because he started drinking guinea corn beer, which is taboo to her. She married Shọpọna, God of Smallpox; but Ọsanyin, God of Medicine, said he would take her by magic. He asked Shọpọna to close his eyes, and before he could open them again Ọsanyin had taken Ọshun away. Ọshun then went to live with Ifa because she wanted to learn how to divine, but once when Ifa was away on a trip, Ọshun cast her sixteen cowries for Ifa's clients even though she had not completed her apprenticeship. When Ifa returned he drove Ọshun from his house, and she taught divination with sixteen cowries to all the deities who wanted to learn, including Orishala and all the white deities, Yemọja, Ọya, Shango, and Eshu, whose worshipers now also use it. She went to live with Orishala, but she left him because he ate snails, which are taboo to her. Finally, because the gods kept fighting over her and because her many children kept bothering her, she turned into a river. Ọshun had children by all her husbands and lovers, but the most children by Orishala. She is as famed for giving children to her worshipers as she is for her beauty, and some claim that her work is to cause conception, creating the fetus which Orishala later shapes into human form.

Shopona, the God of Smallpox

Shopona is the God of Smallpox and a brother of Shango. His worship has been prohibited by the Nigerian Government for many years because of charges that his priests used scabs and liquids to spread smallpox in order to obtain the property of their victims. His shrines are still to be found in Nigeria, however, and many of his worshipers cross the border into Dahomey to perform his annual festival and lesser rituals. They are naturally somewhat reluctant to discuss their cult, but they deny the charges made against them. They admit that evil persons can cause smallpox, not by spreading germs, but by violating his strong taboos against benniseed (sesame seed) and palm kernel oil. Like Eshu, Shopona can be made to fight with an enemy by mentioning his name while placing a tabooed substance on his shrine. They regard this practice as evil, however, and contrary to the very purposes of their cult, which are to prevent the spread of smallpox and to aid in the recovery of those who are suffering from it.

Before the cult was suppressed, the priests of Shopona were called to help when a person was afflicted with smallpox. They prayed and offered sacrifices and sprinkled the patient and his room with an infusion of leaves. If the patient recovered, the priests made an atonement or "cooling" to prevent a recurrence and the family gave a feast. During the illness the patient and his relatives observed the taboos of Shopona to avoid angering him and thus spreading the affliction to others in the house. The house could not be swept with the traditional broom or besom made of the mid-ribs of palm leaves, because a similar broom is one of his symbols; the stems of *Sida* leaves were used instead. It is a taboo to burn corncobs or wood of the ashapa tree, as both of these are liked by Shopona and used in preventing smallpox. Most important, benniseed and palm kernel oil must not be brought into the house.

When a person died of small pox no funeral rites were performed and the body was not buried in the house. Shopona's priests were called to make an atonement and to sprinkle the infusion of leaves on the relatives who carried the body deep into the bush where the grave would not be seen. The priests collected all of the deceased's clothing and personal property, except money, and burned them or buried them with the body.

Smallpox is not considered a disease, but a punishment by Shopona for those who offend him by whistling, by laughing at him when he possesses a worshiper, or by breaking his other taboos. Shopona is greatly feared because he is ruthless; once smallpox starts it can spread to innocent people and in earlier times it could kill half the people in town. He is a thief who steals the souls of those he kills and sells them in distant towns to women to whom they are reborn as children. If he returns a soul to its owner, the sick person may refuse food and drink, saying that he has already had them, although he has been lying unconscious for several days.

Shopona lives deep in the forest during the rainy season, but he may come to town during the dry season when the worst smallpox epidemics occur, often manifesting himself as a whirlwind, "a wind that walks like a man." During the dry season one should be careful not to go out at midday or at night. At night he goes out to fight, accompanied by his dogs and by small evil spirits who carry cudgels and whips; and at midday he and his followers hide in the shade of a tree, where one may be tempted to rest from the sun. He loves music and drumming, which may attract him into the town, so that when the dry season begins or when smallpox enters a town, all drumming may be prohibited. Despite the suppression of his cult, despite conversions to Islam and Christianity, and despite vaccination campaigns, drumming was prohibited in Oyo, Meko, and other towns in the fall of 1950, and the planting of benniseed near town was still prohibited for fear of offending Shopona. Little if any benniseed is grown by the Yoruba, although it is one of Nigeria's commercial exports.

The shrine for Shopona contains an inverted pot with a broken hole at the top, beneath which are two iron standards to which the blood of sacrificial animals is fed. There is also an iron spear, a forked iron staff, and a wooden cudgel reddened with camwood. In place of a fly whisk or dance wand the worshippers use a besom whose handle is covered with cloth or leather and decorated with cowry shells, the whole being reddened with camwood. Bracelets of cowry shells and necklaces of small black discs made from palm nut shells are worn as his insignia.

Because he is feared, the name Shopona is avoided. Instead he is referred to simply as "Father" (Baba) or "Lord" (Oluwa), or by one of his many praise names. He is called "King in the Forest" or "Father in the Forest" (Obaligbo, Babaligbo), "Child of the Lord" (Omolu) and "King, Lord of the World" or "Father, Lord of the World" (Obaluaiye, Babaluaiye). If you remember the once very popular Cuban song which began "Babalu, Babalu, Babaluaiye," you may be surprised to know that it was about the Yoruba God of Smallpox.

Ogboni and Oro

The Ogboni cult was mentioned earlier in Chapter 4 because of its judicial functions, but it also has another role, devoted to the worship of Ogboni as the Earth God and son of Odua. Among the favorite foods of the deity are steamed beans, yam loaves, kola nuts, pigeons, and rams, which are fed him through the Ogboni symbols laid on the ground. The principal taboos are that human blood must not be shed on the ground, a member must not address a fellow member by his personal name or reveal what takes place in the Ogboni house, and nonmembers must not enter the Ogboni house. However, many of the special "passwords" or greetings and the special handshakes of the Ogboni are common knowledge, as is membership in the cult; in fact, its members wear a metal chain or a leather cord on their wrist as their insignia.

When I was initiated into the Ogboni cult, some of the members were concerned that I might reveal their secrets and publish photographs of their rituals. However the Oni, who supported my admission, said that it would not matter if I did. He reminded them of the many photographs that they had seen of the coronation of King George VI the year before,* and asked if they understood what was really happening. When they admitted that they did not, he argued that neither would anyone who saw any pictures that I might take, and he was right. My regular interpreter was not admitted to the Ogboni house, and I did not find a member who could serve adequately in his place. Although I attended the meetings regularly, most of what I learned about the Ogboni was learned outside.

The Oro cult also had political functions, although Oro is worshiped as a deity who was a follower of Eleshije, the Ife God of Medicine, and the one who taught people the use of the bullroarer. The priests of Oro are called to make atonement at the death of a man afflicted by elephantiasis of the testicles, and, in former times, they could be delegated to dispose of a person guilty of witchcraft or making bad medicine. Then the roar of the bullroarers would be heard in town, and the guilty person would be carried away; later he would be found hanging from the top of a high tree wearing only his waist cloth, with the rest of his clothing scattered about in the tree top. During the Oro festivals in Oyo and Iseyin, the Oro worshipers, joined by many young boys, whirl their bullroarers in town while all the women and girls stay in their houses behind closed doors and the markets are deserted. However, in Ife the women do not have to stay inside during Oro festivals because the bullroarers are whirled in Oro's sacred grove outside of town. Oro did not enter Ife except to make atonements, to dispose of offenders, or to execute an unwanted king. Oro's favorite foods include cornstarch, seasoned mashed yams, yam loaves, boiled corn and beans, cocks, rams, and he-goats. His principal taboo is that women must not see the bullroarers.

Egungun, Gelede, and Epa

The Egungun cult is dedicated to the worship of Amaiyegun, the god who taught people how to make and use the costumes which mask their wearers, and thus saved the people of Ife when Death and his followers were killing them. His favorite foods include he-goats and she-goats, rams and ewes, and cocks and hens. His taboos include dogs, cats, tortoises, snails, and snakes. Women must not know the identity of the man concealed in the costume; and if they should recognize their husband or their brother, they must not say so. It is also taboo for a worshiper to reveal this secret to a woman, or to put ordinary food in the shrine where sacrifices are offered.

There are four quite different classes of Egungun. The "elder Egungun" which is the most powerful and most feared, wears a costume of dirty rags to which many charms have been tied, and carries on his head a mask carved of wood or an amorphous mass of clay inset with monkey skulls and smeared with the blood and oil of many sacrifices. Like Oro, the elder Egungun formerly executed witches and workers of bad magic, presumably because they were too dangerous to be apprehended by the secular Ogungbe, and assisted in the execution of the king. The "children of Egungun," which are the most numerous, dress in fine costumes with panels of appliquéd cloth and leather to which mirrors are some-

times attached. Followed by many women whose praise and admiration they seek, they dance about town during the Egungun festival with their panels whirling out from their bodies, like those of the mount of Shango. A third class (Egungun alago) wears a long, trailing, bag-like costume which represents a shroud. It is made at the instruction of a babalawo to honor a relative who has recently died, and the worshiper wears the costume during the annual festival, walking and talking like the deceased. Finally, the "trickster Egungun" have elaborate costumes representing various animals in which they appear, amusing the spectators and astonishing them with rapid changes and magical disappearances; they also have numerous wooden masks with which they mimic various peoples and occupations. In Ifẹ this last class is regarded as a class of beggars or professional entertainers of no religious significance, and is said to have been introduced from Ọyọ.

Gẹlẹdẹ is another deity for whom masks are worn by men, but there is no secrecy about their identity. This cult, which is restricted to the western Yoruba (Ketu, Shabẹ, Ifọnyin, and Ẹgbado), is also concerned with witches, but rather than executing them, its members propitiate the witches by offering sacrifices. In fact, Gẹlẹdẹ herself is believed to have been a witch when she lived on earth. "Witches" are human; they are old women who have small birds or cats as animal familiars into which their souls can enter to go out at night and give a person a disease or suck his blood while he sleeps. The sacrifices are offered to Gẹlẹdẹ with prayers that she will keep the witches from harming others. Her favorite foods include seasoned mashed yams, cornstarch gruel, cornstarch porridge, kola nuts, maize beer, hens, and she-goats. A fire must not be lit in her shrine, and she must not be fed any male bird or animal, palm kernel oil, cats, dogs, tortoises, or snakes.

Large helmet masks are worn by men in the festival of Ẹpa, again with no secrecy about their identity. Ẹpa is a male deity who was once a woodcarver. His cult, which is restricted to the northern Yoruba (northern Ekiti and southern Igbomina), is not particularly concerned with witches according to the literature, but only with the general welfare of his worshipers. During his festival, which is held every other year, the masked dancers must jump onto a large flat-topped mound about 3 feet high. As some Ẹpa masks are 4 feet tall and weigh up to at least 60 pounds, this is no easy feat; and if it is accomplished without accident, this is a sign that Ẹpa accepts the sacrifice that has been offered. The masked

(a) An "elder Egungun" at Igana, 1938. A baboon or monkey skull is embedded in a mass of clay or some other substance, which is studded with cowry shells and covered with the dried blood of sacrificial animals. Note the jaw bone hanging at the front.

(b) A "trickster Egungun," named Marikoto, representing a small snail (okoto), Mẹko, 1950. The costume is completely covered with real snail shells, which make a tinkling sound in dancing, and a carved wooden snail sits on top of the head.

(c) Two "trickster Egungun" masks, used to parody a "Gambari" (Hausa) on the left, and a "Tapa" (Nupe) on the right. Mẹko, 1950.

Gẹlẹdẹ at Mẹkọ, 1950. The one at the left represents a petty trader named
Adẹpatẹ selling things like kola nuts, guinea peppers, and matches. The one at the
right represents Ẹfẹ, her husband.

dancers are followed by stilt dancers who perform feats of agility; stilt dancers and masks also appear in the festivals of a few other deities. The taboos of Epa have not been recorded, but his favorite foods include dogs, cocks, and bean fritters.

It is hoped that this highly selective discussion will at least suggest the complexity, and the regional variability, of Yoruba religion. For each of the hundreds of deities there are appropriate songs, dances, rhythms, musical instruments, taboos, praise names, insignia, shrine carvings and other paraphernalia, leaves, sacrificial foods, and symbols through which they are fed. The Yoruba are explicit that it is not these material symbols which are being worshiped, but rather the deities that they represent. The myths recount the relationships between the deities, their fights and love affairs, the specific towns from which they are believed to have come, and the places where they became gods when they "went into the ground," "rose into the sky," "became a river," or "turned into stone." Over fifty deities are identified with specific hills, there is a series of river gods and goddesses, and other deities manifest themselves as winds, snakes, or insects. Many others, however, like Odua, Orishala, Ifa, and Eshu, are not "nature gods." The deities are often described as having distinctive roles and individual personalities, or as "owning" certain materials such as brass or iron. All can punish those who offend or neglect them by causing illness and misfortune, and some have special ways of "fighting" with people. The priests of some deities are called upon to perform the atonement for anyone who dies in a special way, whether or not he was a worshiper, so that a similar death will not recur in his family.

Except for Olorun, the deities have their own initiation rites, atonements which are performed before a worshiper is buried, and annual festivals which last a week or so. At these festivals the worshipers gather to sing and dance, feast and drink, offer sacrifices, and pray that they may live to perform the festival again next year. All the deities can give children, so it is misleading to speak of individual gods or goddesses of fertility. All can aid their worshipers by giving them good health and prosperity, and by helping them to achieve their destinies and live out their allotted spans of life on earth.

9

Esthetics

Verbal Art, Music, and the Dance

YORUBA VERBAL ARTS INCLUDE praise names, praise poems, tongue twist-
ers, hundreds of prose narratives and riddles, and thousands of proverbs.
Of the prose narratives, myths about the deities and legends about past
kings and war heroes are grouped together in a single category; both are considered
to be factual accounts of past events, in contrast to folktales which are recognized
as fiction. Tortoise, the crafty, greedy trickster in the folktales occasionally appears
in myths about the deities. Whether the principal characters are humans or animals, the folktales are predominantly moralistic in intent; whereas the myths and
legends impart information that is important because it is regarded as true.

An evening session of telling folktales is usually preceded by a riddling
contest among the children. Riddles are recognized as sharpening the wits and
training the memory of children; but they also impart knowledge; for example,
that a commoner may not eat with the king, touch his head, or pass his palace without greeting him. Yoruba riddles are usually phrased as declarative sentences, rather
than as questions, and the implicit question to be answered may not be readily
apparent to an outsider; for example, "It bears fruit, we cannot pick it; the fruit
falls, we cannot gather it." Answer: "Dew."

Riddles are considered to be meant for children, but proverbs are the con-
cern of adults, and a boy must ask permission before quoting a proverb in the
presence of adults. Because they express Yoruba morals and ethics, they are con-
venient standards for appraising behavior, and they are continually quoted in
discussing an issue and in commenting on the behavior of others. They are used
to express social approval and disapproval; praise for those who conform to accepted social conventions and criticism, or ridicule of those who deviate; warning,
defiance, or derision of an enemy or rival, and advice, counsel, or warning to a
friend, when either contemplates action which may lead to social friction, open
hostilities, or direct punishment. The proverb, "However small the needle, a

chicken cannot swallow it" conveys the message that an apparently weaker individual can cause unexpected difficulties for a more powerful rival. It can be used to warn or defy a more powerful enemy to treat the speaker more respectfully; to warn or advise a friend to change his behavior toward a rival who seems weaker; or to ridicule and criticise someone whose behavior toward a weaker person has brought trouble on himself. Proverbs are highly regarded because of the wisdom they express; it is significant that although even sacred myths have been questioned in the post-contact period, educated Yoruba have retained their respect for proverbs.

There are also songs of ridicule and songs of praise, as well as lullabies, religious songs, war songs, and work songs. These usually follow the common call and response pattern by the leader and chorus. Yoruba music also shares the African characteristics of dominance of rhythm and percussion, polymeter, and off-beat phrasing. Rhythm is provided by a variety of drum sets, iron gongs and cymbals, rattles, and hand clapping. Other instruments include long brass trumpets, side-blown ivory trumpets, whistles, stringed instruments, and metallophones. Each deity has its own songs and an appropriate set of drums, rhythm, and manner of dancing. Yoruba dancing is sedate and dignified, and, with the exception of stilt dancing, less spectacular than that of some other West African peoples.

Perhaps the most interesting musical instrument is the West African pressure or "talking" drum. Yoruba is a tonal language; the same combination of vowels and consonants has different meanings depending upon the pitch of the vowels, for example, a cymbal (aro), indigo dye (aró), lamentation (arò), and a granary (àró). The pressure drum has a wooden body shaped like an hour glass, and two leather heads joined by leather cords laced back and forth between them. It is carried on a shoulder strap and can be tuned instantaneously by pressing on the cords with the elbow; and it "speaks" by reproducing the pitch of the vowels, while a suggestion of the sound of some consonants can be given by fingering the drum head. Pressure drums are used by professional drummers to provide rhythmical accompaniment for singing and dancing, and to "speak" the praise names of chiefs and other important individuals. The melody of the sentence can also be reproduced by the trumpets, which are used in praising Yoruba kings.

Bodily Decoration

Of the visual arts, some, like bodily decoration, clothing, pottery, carved calabashes, leatherwork, and carved wooden spoons and mirror cases are available to all who can afford them. A few items, such as the weaver's carved wooden heddle pulley and the iron poker topped by a human figure cast in brass, which a blacksmith sent with his messenger to authenticate his message, are appropriate for special occupations. Others, like beaded clothing, are reserved to the kings; and most, but by no means all, are associated with the worship of the deities.

Facial and body scarification, although symbols of clan affiliation, are also a means of beautification. So also is the use of ground galena to darken the out-

lines of women's eyes, rubbing of the body with palm kernel oil and camwood pow-
der, and the former practice of chipping an M-shaped notch between the upper
incisors. Jewelry is also used as a means of decoration, including red stone lip
plugs which were formerly worn by northern Yoruba women.

Hairdress is an important form of decoration for women. The hair of
men and elderly women is often shaved close, but younger women's hair is dressed
in various ways. The most easily described forms are composed of parallel, tightly
braided stripes running from the forehead to the back of the head where they end
in a row of tiny queues, from the back of the head to the forehead, from the top
of the head downward and ending in a circle of tiny queues, and from the hairline
to the top of the head ending in a small topknot. Some priests of Shango and
Orishala wear their hair braided like women, and other special forms of hairdress,
including a high ridge of hair in the center of the head which is often depicted
in woodcarvings, are worn by worshipers of other deities. Many of these religious styles are rapidly disappearing, but in the years since World War II a whole
series of new hair styles for women have been introduced.

Weaving and Clothing

Of equal importance to hair dress is the cloth head tie by which Yoruba
women can often be recognized. This is a rectangular piece of cloth which is tied
about the head in a number of imaginative ways, with new fashions still being
created. Another rectangular cloth, tied about the waist, serves to support a child
carried on its mother's back. A third such cloth may be worn over the shoulder
as a shawl, and Bowen reported that this and the head tie were all that were worn
above the waist in the last century; in this century, however, a loose-fitting, short-
sleeved blouse has become a standard garment. A larger rectangular cloth serves
as a wrap-around skirt.

Men wear tailored cloth hats, gowns, and trousers of several different patterns. A popular form of gown is shaped like a poncho; it reaches to the fingertips
but is worn folded back on the shoulders. Trousers are usually very loose and
baggy. European styles of dress have become common for both men and women,
but traditional clothing is still worn on important occasions.

Both men and women weave, using different types of looms. Women weave
on the vertical "mat loom," which resembles that of the Navajo Indians, producing
a cloth about 2 feet wide and 7 feet long. Men weave on the horizontal narrow-band
treadle loom, which produces a strip of cloth only 3 to 4 inches wide but as long
as may be needed; the long strips are cut to the desired length and sewn together
to make clothing. In both cases lengthwise patterns predominate, being laid down
in the warp; but weft patterns can also be made, using two shuttles with different
colored threads. Patterns are named, often after the clubs which first ordered them.
Club members often wear identical garments so that they can be recognized when
they go through the streets, and some clubs purchase new outfits every year. Securing the order of a club of a hundred or more members is obviously important to
a weaver, and one of his motivations for creating new patterns. Several hundred

different patterns are woven on the men's loom alone in Ọyọ and Iseyin, two of the important weaving centers.

Cloth is woven from wild silk and from locally grown cotton. A mixture of cotton threads and raphia is also woven into cloth, but is not used for clothing. Cotton is ginned on a wooden block using an iron roller to squeeze out the seeds. It is then fluffed on a bow string, spun with a simple spindle, and rewound into skeins ready for dyeing.

Dyeing and Embroidery

The most popular dye is indigo, which produces varying shades ranging from a light sky blue to a purplish blue-black, depending upon the number of batches of dye used. Imported indigo has long been available, but it is considered inferior to that produced locally. There were also red and yellow dyes, a tan dye to imitate the more expensive wild silk, and the natural white and tan colors of light and dark cotton. Imported red, yellow, tan, and black dyes are commonly used, and imported thread is used for cheaper cloths, which do not last as long as those made with the coarser homespun threads. Ginning, fluffing, spinning, rewinding, and dyeing are done by women.

Women also do resist-dyeing, using indigo dye and imported cotton sheeting, and producing patterns of quite different types from those woven on the loom. Small seeds or pebbles are tied tightly into the cloth with raphia; or folds in the cloth are sewed with raphia or on sewing machines; or the cloth is twisted tightly; or cornstarch or cassava starch is painted on the cloth through holes cut in a stencil. The tying, sewing, twisting, or starching protects portions of the cloth from the dye, producing patterns in contrasting blue and white. The city of Abẹokuta is a major center of resist-dyeing.

Men do embroidery, particularly on the large gowns worn by men and on men's caps. Men are also the tailors and dressmakers, and the ones who use hand-operated sewing machines. Floor mats, mat bags for storing clothing (and formerly cowries), baskets, and basketry sieves and strainers are also made.

Sculpture in cement adorns many graves and private homes. Wall painting in geometric and representational patterns decorates some shrines and tombs; but aside from these, painted designs were rare in former times. The palaces of kings and town chiefs (Balẹ) are distinguished by frontal platforms of mud covered by a gabled roof that was higher than the rest of the building. Formerly no other house in town could be taller than this, but early in this century separate, two-story houses became popular as a sign of wealth.

Pottery and Calabash Carving

Women are the potters. In addition to palm oil lamps and some twenty kinds of pots and dishes for cooking, eating, carrying and storing liquids, and other daily uses, potters say that there is a special kind of pot for each of the hundreds of deities. These are sometimes decorated with sculptural forms, whereas daily ware is decorated with cord markings or red trim. Most pottery is brown ware, but black ware is preferred for eating, and ritual pottery is sometimes colored with red, white, or blue pigments. Pottery is not done everywhere; quite naturally towns with nearby sources of good clay produce pottery for export to other towns. In ancient Ifẹ, clay was important as a medium for terra-cotta sculpture.

Gourds or calabashes are also used for drinking, serving food, and carrying palm wine, sacrifices, and goods to sell in the market. Some are used as containers for the ingredients of "medicines," and others are made into rattles. Some calabashes are decorated with carved geometric or representational designs, Ọyọ being a major center of this activity. The calabash carvers are a group of men who are distinct from the woodcarvers.

Leatherworking and Beadworking

Leatherworking is done by men, and Ọyọ is a major center of this activity. Sheep, goat, and antelope skins are made into cushions, fans, bags, saddles and saddlery, knife sheaths, sandals, hunter's fly whisks, shoulder straps and end ornaments of pressure drums, and other items. White, black, red, yellow, green, and blue leather is produced. Appliquéd designs are made by sewing together different colored pieces of leather, and other patterns are made by cutting through the colored surface to reveal the natural color of the leather. Besides secular items, the leatherworkers make the shoulder bags (laba) carried by Shango priests, their leather covered gourd rattles, and the appliquéd panels of the costumes of the "children of Egungun."

Beadworking is also done by men, often under royal patronage. They produce the crowns, caps, and other solidly beaded pieces used by the kings and the babalawo, although some babalawo do their own beadwork. Common motifs in royal beadworking are the interwoven design found also in embroidery and woodcarving, human faces with clan facial marks, three dimensional birds which were appended to some crowns, and, more recently, floral designs. The babalawo's beaded bags may depict full human figures, men on horseback, and such objects as guns, crowns, and divining trays. Trade beads imported from Europe are most often used; but coral, red stone beads, and a highly prized tubular blue bead (ṣegi) were probably of African origin. Crucible fragments coated with glass of blue and other colors, glass droppings, and glass beads have been excavated at Ifẹ, indicating that it was a center of the glass making industry in precontact times.

Metal Working

Blacksmiths produce hoes, axes, adzes, machetes (known locally as cutlasses), knives, swords, traps, shackles, chains, bells and gongs, the specialized knives and scrapers of the calabash carvers, the iron tools of the leatherworkers, and their own hammers, tongs, pincers, pokers, chisels, and knives and adzes for dressing wooden tool handles. In addition to these utilitarian objects they fashioned the iron necklaces worn by some Ogun worshipers and the sixteen miniature iron objects attached to them: a blacksmith's hammer, tongs, and poker, a hoe, a bell, a gong, a knife, a double-edged knife, a cutlass, a king's sword of state, a deity's sword, a dagger, a spear, a tool used in cutting facial marks, a hook-like scraper used in working calabashes, and a symbol of Osanyin, the Oyo God of Medicine. They also fashion the full scale symbol of Osanyin (an iron standard surmounted by sixteen birds); the iron standard and chain bracelet of Erinle; a lamp supported by an iron horseman for some shrines of Ogun and Shango; a snake-like form representing lightning for the shrine of Agbona, the Ketu God of Thunder; a miniature iron bow and arrow for the shrine of Oshosi, a Hunter God; and rings, bracelets, and human figures in iron which were used in charms. Sculpture in forged iron is not common in Africa, but it is also produced by the Fon of Dahomey, and the Dogon and Bambara of Mali. Before scrap iron became available, the smiths bought iron from the men who smelted it locally; but there has been no iron smelting since about 1920. Blacksmiths are found in almost every town, but Iseyin was a major center of ironworking.

Some blacksmiths also engage in brass working, producing rings, bracelets, small knives, swords and sword handles, bells for pressure drums, vials in which "medicine" is kept, human figures used in charms, Ogboni symbols, and "messenger pokers" for their own use. Brass is drawn into wire and then bent over and pounded together to make needles. It is beaten to produce simple rings and bracelets, the symbols of Oshun, and the fans and knives with which Oshun worshipers dance. Some rings are cast in impressions made in cuttlefish shells, but the more complex forms are cast by the lost wax (*cire perdue*) process.

The form is first modeled in beeswax and coated with clay. Two or more wax stems are left extended from the wax figure to the outer edge of the clay. When the clay has dried, it is heated and the melted wax is poured out through the vent formed by one of the stems. After all the wax has been volatilized by further heating, molten metal is poured through a vent into the hollow mold left by the wax figure. Each object is produced from a separate wax original, as the mold is destroyed when the clay coating is broken away after the metal has cooled. In principle the method is simple; but in practice it requires great skill.

The famous Ife heads of the precontact period were cast in this manner after first building up a thin layer of beeswax on a modeled clay core. The source of brass at this period is still not known, although copper ore has been found on the southern edge of the Sahara and both tin and zinc are mined in Nigeria. Brass casting continued in Ife into the twentieth century, but in a very different sculptural style. In 1937 I saw the "messenger pokers" made by the head blacksmith, Gbetu of Ile Okiti, by his father, and by his grandfather. Imported brass was exclusively used at that time. Imported copper and lead are also cast or pounded into similar objects, and several of the Ife heads are almost pure copper. Some blacksmiths cast or work coin silver and imported gold into jewelry, and there are other men who specialize in goldsmithing.

Woodcarving

The woodcarvers are also men. Their two most important tools are the adze, with which sculptural forms are fashioned, and the knife, which is used in finishing the surface and in carving incised patterns. Both sculpture and geometrical designs are considered as art (ọna); and those who "carve art" (gbẹ-ọna-gbẹ-ọna) in making masks and figurines are distinguished from those who simply "carve wood" (gbẹ-igi-gbẹ-igi) into mortars, pestles, and utilitarian bowls. The former are also known as "those who make art" (onishọna), along with the embroiderers and leatherworkers.

Of all the visual arts, woodcarving accounts for the greatest variety of decorated and sculptural forms. A chicken may perch on a weaver's pulley or on the handle of a carved spoon, and human figures may be on the top of a mirror case. The playing boards for the cup game (ayo) called warri or mancala are sometimes supported by standing figures. Twin figures are carved at the death of twins. Palace and shrine doors are covered with human and other forms carved in low or high relief, and the roofs of chiefs' houses are supported by posts which are carved to represent horsemen, cyclists, and standing or kneeling figures, sometimes with one figure perched on another.

A similar column of figures is carved on the handle of the spear-like staff kept in the shrines of Yewa, a River Goddess, and Iroko, a deity whose role is to make peace when Eshu has caused a fight; the priest of Yewa also uses a wooden shield with a face carved in low relief. Carved stools are used during the initiation ceremonies of the cults of Yewa, Iroko, and other deities; and an inverted mortar decorated in low relief is similarly used in the Shango cult and as the stand on which the bowl of his thunderstones is set. Shango's mount dances holding a carved wand (oshe Shango) which is often in the form of a human figure surmounted

(a) *Duga, master carver of Mẹkọ, carving a Shango dance wand (oshe Shango). 1950. This is a copy of the central dance wand (see p. 85), which its owner did not wish to sell. The central figure represents a "mount" of Shango, carrying an oshe Shango in his right hand. His left hand rests on a female worshiper of Ọya, Goddess of the River Niger and Shango's most loyal wife, who is giving the traditional greeting of Ọya's worshipers to Shango's mount. The man at the other side is beating Shango's drum (bata). The top, which usually represents two "thunderstones," has been elaborated into a frame for a ram at the left and a dog at the right. The ram is Shango's favorite sacrificial animal, and there is a dog which is sacred to him (p. 87).*

(b) *A man's loom at Mẹkọ, 1950. The weaver holds the shuttle in his left hand, and in his right the reed with which he battens down the weft thread. The two heddles which separate the warp threads are operated by his feet.*

(c) *A leather worker using a hammer to flatten the appliquéd top of a leather cushion at Ọyo, 1951.*

by a representation of two thunderstones in the form of a double-bladed axe. Blackened wands from which strings of cowry shells are suspended and which are topped by human figures are carried by the devotees of Eshu when they are begging for money; some wear a larger carved figure with the long queue distinctive of their deity hooked over their shoulder; and some carry a blackened wooden fan with geometric decorations and often with the handle in the form of a human figure. The worshipers of Ẹrinlẹ wear on their shoulder a hunter's fly whisk, the handle of which is carved in human form. The shrines of Ẹrinlẹ, Yemọja, Shango, Ogun and other deities are adorned with carved figures which are given as votive offerings by their worshipers.

Ifa diviners use rectangular, circular, or semi-circular wooden trays whose raised borders are carved, usually in low relief, with the face of Eshu and various combinations of animal figures and geometric patterns. The Ifa bell or tapper is of wood, ivory, or brass, shaped like a small tusk and often with a human figure at the other end. The cups in which babalawo store Ifa's sacred palm nuts are carved to represent a wide variety of animal forms and human activities, including a chicken biting a snake that is striking back at the chicken's leg, an antelope, dried fish, a mother of twins, a kneeling woman offering a sacrifice, a woman weaving, a chief on horseback surrounded by his attendants, and a babalawo engaged in divining.

The large standing drums used by the Ogboni are often covered with relief carvings, and the smaller ones used for Orishala and the other "white deities" are sometimes supported by human figures carved as part of the drum. Some Oro cults have a large wooden bullroarer which is decorated with figures carved in relief.

Masks are used in the Egungun, Gẹlẹdẹ, Ẹpa and several other cults. The carved masks of the "elder Egungun" are usually worn perched on top of the head with the face covered by a netting which forms part of the attached costume. These carvings represent such things as a monkey's or a rabbit's head, a snail, the head of an Eshu worshiper, or simply a woman's hairdress. The masks of the "trickster Egungun," which are simply for amusement, are worn flat against the face; the wearer uses appropriate clothing and paraphernalia to parody a Nupe, a Hausa, a white man, a hunter, a sanitary inspector, a policeman, a produce buyer, a Shango worshiper, an Ifa diviner, or a harlot in comic burlesques. Gẹlẹdẹ masks, which appear in pairs, often identical, are worn resting on top of the head and slanting down over the top of the face; they represent such things as roosters, rams, drummers, Egungun dancers, truck drivers, airplanes, and petty traders selling kola nuts,

(a) *A carved calabash from Ọyọ. It is used for serving food and is decorated all over with birds.*

(b) *A Yoruba mirror case, exact provenance unknown. The cover swings open like a door to reveal the mirror behind it.*

(c) *A forged iron symbol of Ọsanyin, the God of Medicine, at Ọyọ, 1951. Sixteen small birds surround a large bird in the center. Shown here with a Yoruba floor mat in the background, this symbol is normally stuck into the ground at Ọsanyin's shrine.*

guinea peppers, cigarettes, and matches. Ẹpa masks have an abstract Janus-faced head with large eyes and a wide, rectangular mouth; this head fits over the wearer's head like a helmet, and is surmounted by a figure or group of figures in a more naturalistic style representing a leopard, a ram, a dog, a priestess of Oshun with her attendants, a priest of Osanyin with his assistants, a mother of twins, or a warrior on horseback surrounded by dozens of followers. The "elder Egungun" dancers see through the netting, the "trickster Egungun" and the Gẹlẹdẹ dancers through the eyeholes of the mask, and the Ẹpa dancers through the open mouth.

Many Yoruba carvings are polychrome. Black, white, tan, red in three shades, green, blue, and pastel blue and pink are made by the carvers from wood, leaves, seeds, and earth pigments. These are naturally matte, but all of them can be made glossy by the addition of a tree gum. The bodies of human figures are often reddened with camwood and their hair is colored blue with commercial bluing. Imported oil paints have been used for many years.

Some Yoruba woodcarvers also carve in bone, ivory, and stone. Elephant bone is used for some of the specialized equipment of the babalawo, ivory for some of their bells or tappers and for elaborately carved armlets, and bone or ivory for the symbols of the "white deities." Whether wood, bone, or ivory is used depends upon the size of the object and what the customer can afford. The 17 foot tall granite column studded with spiral-headed iron nails, known as the staff of Oranmiyan, is one of the striking antiquities of Ife, but there are also smaller columns and carved stone figures of humans, snakes, fish, and crocodiles, presumably from the same period. As late as 1938, carving in soft stone was done in Ife, and I commissioned a woodcarver to make for me a small steatite figurine (esi) of the type that is buried at the town gate to protect the welfare of the town. The carving of granite, and the even more remarkable fashioning of quartz into large stools, belong to the classical period of Ife's history.

It is not possible, nor is it necessary, to mention all of the art forms produced by the Yoruba. They have been called "the largest and most prolific of the art-producing tribes of Africa." This claim may sound extreme but it is not much, if any, of an exaggeration. Few African peoples surpass them in numbers, and they certainly have produced a large quantity and a wide array of sculpture and other visual arts in addition to their wealth of verbal art and music.

(a) *A pair of brass Ogboni symbols (ẹdan Ogboni) from Ife. Like the brass heads from ancient Ife, they were cast using the cire perdue or "lost wax" process.*

(b) *An ivory Ifa bell or tapper from Mẹko. Before beginning to divine, a babalawo taps the Ifa tray (see p. 87) with it, to call the attention of Ifa, God of Divination. The upper end is hollow, but does not have a clapper as some do.*

(c) *A wooden spoon, topped by a cock, from Mẹko.*

(d) *A pair of twin figures from Oyo. Each wears beads around the neck, waist, and right wrist, and a white metal bracelet on the left wrist. Note the size of the head in relation to the torso and legs.*

Yoruba Style

Several features of Yoruba style deserve comment. Most African sculpture consists of a single figure or a pair of figures, such as mother and child; group compositions of several figures are not common. However, groups of several figures are found on a number of Yoruba stools, doors, game boards, shrine ornaments, Ifa cups, and Ẹpa masks. In carving groups of figures, the importance of the main figure is emphasized by reducing—sometimes quite drastically—the scale of subordinate figures, for example, making a horseman larger than his horse. In a similar fashion the human head is emphasized, probably because of its association with luck and destiny, with the result that the human figure is commonly portrayed as composed of three parts of approximately equal size, head, torso, and legs. Compared to many African cultures, Yoruba carving is relatively naturalistic and restrained, and for this reason, has not been appreciated by those who prefer the abstract or the grotesque. Regional variations in the style of carving can be distinguished, identifying such sub-styles as Ketu, Ẹgba, Ọyọ, and Ekiti, and the hand of an individual artist can even be recognized; but there is a basic stylistic unity in Yoruba woodcarving. On the other hand, the style of Yoruba woodcarving is distinct from that of Yoruba calabash carving, brass casting, forged iron work, pottery, beadwork, leatherwork, weaving, and resist-dyeing.

Art is obviously important to Yoruba religion, but no carvings or other paraphernalia are made for Ọlọrun, the Sky God. Two stone figures in the main shrine of Orishala in Ifẹ are said to be Orishala and his wife, Yemo; and a few of the Ifẹ heads have been retrospectively attributed as being deities. However, with the exception of Eshu, whose face appears on the Ifa trays, no woodcarvings or recent brasscastings represent the deities. Rather, they represent their worshipers, and often the individuals who gave them as votive offerings. An eighty-year-old priest once pointed out a carving on his shrine for Yemọja, depicting his mother carrying him as a baby on her back, which his mother had given in thanks when he was born.

(a) *A stool for Iroko, a deity who makes peace when Eshu causes a fight, from Mẹkọ. The priestess in the center holds the sacrificial knife in her right hand, and with the other she holds the hand of a novitiate. A drummer is seated at the left, and above are two pythons which support the seat.*

(b) *An Ifa cup for storing palm nuts, from Ẹfọn Alaye. The head, back, and tail of the cock serve as the lid. Note the facial marks, the high crest of the woman's hair dress, and how the small figures at the base are subordinated to the woman and her sacrificial cock.*

(c) *A playing board for the cup game (ayo), from Ijẹbu-Rẹmọ. Twelve small figures support the two rows of six cups through which the seed counters are moved. This widespread game is played with varying rules throughout Africa and as far distant as the Philippines.*

These and other carvings are recognized as contributing aesthetically to the shrines which they adorn and the rituals in which they are used. It has sometimes been maintained that, although Africans respected their sculptures as religious objects, they did not regard them as art or evaluate them in aesthetic terms. At least as far as the Yoruba are concerned, this is not true. Many of these sculptures are not essential to the worship of the deities. A babalawo does not need a carved cup in which to store his palm nuts; a simple dish will suffice. What is indispensable are the symbols through which the deities are fed: the 16 palm nuts of Ifa, the river-worn pebbles of Yemoja, Erinle, and Oshun, and the thunderstones of Shango and Oya.

Moreover, in a lengthy, detailed, and important investigation, Robert Farris Thompson isolated nineteen different factors, including symmetry, delicacy, and skill, by which Yoruba woodcarvings are judged. His critics preferred figures which portrayed people at the prime of life and whose details were readily visible, while criticising others because the nose was placed too high on the face or the thighs were too thick. Thompson found that both carvers and owners are reluctant to evaluate their own pieces, esthetically, but that in terms of fluency and speed of verbalization some Yoruba farmers surpass all but the more polished western observers.

10

Postscript

YORUBA ARTS HAVE CHANGED, like all other aspects of Yoruba culture. Weavers, dyers, blacksmiths, leatherworkers, and potters continue to produce, despite the stiff competition of factory goods imported from Europe, India, and Japan. However, because it was so intimately associated with religion, the art of sculpture has suffered. As a result of conversions to Christianity and Islam, woodcarvers and brass casters have lost a large proportion of their customers. Their work has become economically unattractive, and it is increasingly difficult for them to find apprentices, as young men prefer to seek jobs in government or business. In 1960 a carver at Ọyọ complained that his son, who was training under him, could hardly be expected to be a good carver, because he was home from school only a few months during the summer. Many Yoruba have been taught in mission schools to look down on African sculpture as evidence of ignorance and superstition, and Islam forbids its adherents to make any representations of humans or animals. Many cult objects have been destroyed, and even the elaborately carved palace doors have sometimes been discarded and replaced with "modern" doors fashioned by carpenters. On the other hand, an excellent national museum has been established in Lagos, and Ifẹ has its own museum for its antiquities. Traditional Yoruba carvings have been used in some government buildings, and Father Carroll's book gives an account of his effort to adapt them for use in the Catholic church. At least in Abẹokuta there has been a revival of carving for the tourist trade within the last few years, and there are sculptors and painters who work in the international art tradition.

Change is nothing new to the Yoruba. It has been going on for centuries, beginning long before European contact. Although we cannot at present chart these changes, or those that happened earlier, great changes certainly had to accompany the development and the flowering of ancient Ifẹ, with its rich art in brass, stone, and terra-cotta, and with the suggestion of a very elaborate political and religious ceremonialism. Great changes also marked the end of this period. Again the causes and the sequence of events are unknown, but the end of this great period seems to have come several centuries before the period of warfare described in Chapter 2. One can only speculate as to whether the city of Ifẹ still retained its earlier form when the first defeat by Modakẹkẹ occurred, whether there had been earlier wars and defeats that have been forgotten, whether internal conflicts brought about the decline, or whether Ifẹ gradually atrophied as Ọyọ rose to the height of its military power in the seventeenth and eighteenth centuries.

Whatever the case may be, the fratricidal wars of the nineteenth century brought further changes of a very profound nature throughout Yoruba territory, as we have seen. The end of these wars marked the beginning of direct European contact throughout much of the area, and the beginning of the colonial period. New legal and political institutions were introduced, stores selling imported goods were built, cocoa farming became the way of life in the forest belt, automobile roads and the railroad were built, ports were developed on the coast and airfields were constructed, Christian churches and mission schools were established, and many Yoruba were converted to Islam, against which they had been fighting throughout most of the previous century. Nigeria's first university was established at Ibadan in 1948. In the late 1950s, electricity became widespread and new factories were built to produce cement, textiles, plastics, shoes, suitcases, foam rubber mattresses and cushions, furniture, metal doors and windows, umbrellas, bicycles, and a variety of other products. In 1959 the first television station in Africa began broadcasting from Ibadan.

When independence came, there was every reason to hope for a bright future for Africa's largest nation. The Yoruba were prosperous, with high prices for cocoa and a continuing expansion of industrialization. An automobile assembly plant was built near Lagos. School facilities were expanded, and new universities were established at Ifẹ and Lagos. However, party politics, introduced prior to independence, and tribalism, led to political abuses and to frictions which soon threatened national unity. Even appointments to traditional local titles were contaminated by party rivalry and the Yoruba found themselves divided again, with the lines of division sometimes following those of the nineteenth century. Just before the Western Region's elections in 1965, the atmosphere was clearly forboding; but who could fortell the assassinations and the coup, or the tragic events which followed?

Now, as I write, the civil war in Nigeria still continues. What changes it will bring, aside from its casualties and destruction, I cannot venture to say. Life in Yoruba towns goes on much as before, I am told; but economic development is being delayed and other sacrifices are being made in support of the Federal Government.

I have seen many changes in the twenty-eight years between my first and last visits to Nigeria, but each time I have returned I have felt at home. Despite the new roads, the new buildings, the new factories, it has been the Nigeria I knew; the Yoruba are still the Yoruba. A great many of my informants are dead; but there has usually been a son or daughter who remembered me from before, and who has been willing to take their place. I think that Americans are often prone to overestimate the effects of European contact and economic development.

Remembering what happened in Brazil and Cuba, I am not ready to concede that Yoruba culture is doomed to sudden extinction. Among the many Cuban refugees in the United States today there are worshipers of Oshun and Ifa and Orishala, and I am told that there is now a Shango temple in New York City.

Recommended Reading

AJAYI, J. F. ADE, 1965, *Christian Missions in Nigeria, 1841–1891*. London: Longmans, Green & Co.
An historical account of mission activities among the Yoruba and in other parts of southern Nigeria.

AJAYI, J. F. ADE, and ROBERT S. SMITH, 1964, *Yoruba Warfare in the Nineteenth Century*. New York: Cambridge University Press.
A discussion of weapons, fortifications, tactics, and history, with special emphasis on the Ijaye war, 1860–1865.

BABALOLA, S. A., 1966, *The Content and Form of Yoruba Ijala*. Oxford Library of African Literature. New York: Oxford University Press.
A collection and analysis of Yoruba praise poems to animals, lineages, individuals, and deities.

BASCOM, WILLIAM, 1944, *The Sociological Role of the Yoruba Cult-Group*. Memoirs of the American Anthropological Association, LXIII.
A comparison of religious cult-groups, clubs, and kinship groupings as units in Yoruba social structure.

BASCOM, WILLIAM, 1951, "Yoruba Food" and "Yoruba Cooking," *Africa*, XXI:41–53, 125–137.
Further details on information summarized at the beginning of Chapter 3.

BASCOM, WILLIAM, 1955, "Urbanization among the Yoruba," *The American Journal of Sociology*, LX:446–454.
An assessment of Louis Wirth's definition of the city, based on an investigation of the size, density, permanency, and social heterogeneity of Yoruba communities.

BASCOM, WILLIAM, 1969, *Ifa Divination: Communication between Gods and Men in West Africa*. Bloomington: Indiana University Press.
An analysis of the method of Ifa divination, with a collection of the verses recited by the babalawo.

BAUMANN, MARGARET I., 1929, *Ajapa the Tortoise*. London: A. & C. Black.
A collection of thirty Yoruba folktales.

BEIER, H. U., 1957, "The Story of Sacred Wood Carvings from One Small Yoruba Town," *Nigeria Magazine*, Lagos.
Illustrations and discussions of sculpture for Erinle, Shango, Ifa, Oya, Eshu, Ogboni, Egungun, and other cults, and their use in the "festival of the images" at Ilobu in the kingdom of Oyo.

BIOBAKU, SABURI O., 1957, *The Egba and their Neighbours, 1842–1872*. Oxford Studies in African Affairs. New York: Oxford University Press.
A study of the history of the Egba state in the period following the founding of Abeokuta.

BOWEN, T. J., 1857, *Central Africa*. Charleston: Southern Baptist Publication Society.
A general account by an early, and usually perceptive and reliable observer, who was in Yoruba country from 1850 to 1856.

BURNS, A. C., 1929, *History of Nigeria*. London: George Allen & Unwin.
A general historical study covering the slave trade, exploration, and colonial administration.

CARROLL, KEVIN, 1967, *Yoruba Religious Carving*. London: Geoffrey Chapman.
A well illustrated study of Yoruba woodcarving, including traditional religious

forms and those produced under the author's direction for use by the Catholic church.

CLAPPERTON, HUGH, 1829, *Journal of a Second Expedition into the Interior of Africa.* Philadelphia: Carey, Lea and Carey.

An account of the earliest known expedition to penetrate Yoruba territory, with a description of Old Ọyọ in Chapters I and II. See also Lander.

COKER, G. B. A., 1958, *Family Property among the Yorubas.* London: Sweet & Maxwell.

A lawyer's analysis of the subject, based in large part on orders-in-council, ordinances, statutes, and court cases.

COLEMAN, JAMES S., 1958, *Nigeria. Background to Nationalism.* Berkeley: University of California Press.

The development of the nationalist movement in Nigeria from its beginning to shortly before independence.

DELANO, ISAAC O., 1966, *Owe l'Ẹsin Ọrọ. Yoruba Proverbs.* New York: Oxford University Press.

A collection of 504 proverbs with Yoruba texts, English translations, and examples of the social situations to which they are appropriate.

ELIAS, T. OLAWALE, 1963, *The Nigerian Legal System.* London: Routledge and Kegan Paul. Second (revised) edition; first published in 1954.

A text book of Nigerian law by the Federal Attorney-General and Minister of Justice for Nigeria.

ELLIS, A. B., 1894, *The Yoruba-Speaking Peoples of the Slave Coast of West Africa.* London: Chapman and Hall.

A general account, based in large part on earlier sources.

FROBENIUS, LEO, 1913, *The Voice of Africa,* Vols. I–II. London: Hutchinson & Co.

An account of his discovery of the Ifẹ heads, with general observations and numerous illustrations.

FUJA, ABAYOMI, 1962, *Fourteen Hundred Cowries.* New York: Oxford University Press.

A collection of thirty-one Yoruba folktales.

GALLETTI, R., K. D. S. BALDWIN, and I. O. DINA, 1956, *Nigerian Cocoa Farmers.* New York: Oxford University Press.

A detailed and comprehensive economic survey of cocoa farming among the Yoruba.

IDOWU, E. BỌLAJI, 1961, *Olodumare. God in Yoruba Belief.* London: Longmans, Green & Co.

A study of the place of the Sky God in Yoruba religion.

JOHNSON, SAMUEL, 1920, *The History of the Yorubas.* London: Routledge & Kegan Paul.

A posthumous account of the successive kings of Ọyọ, based in large part on verbal traditions, and of the wars of the nineteenth century, based in part on first hand observation, written from the point of view of the people of Ọyọ.

KAUFMANN, HERBERT, 1962, *Nigeria.* Die Länder Afrikas, Band 3. Bonn: Kurt Schroeder. Second (enlarged) edition. First published in 1958.

A general book about Nigeria, with background material and a description of the country shortly after independence.

KOPYTOFF, JEAN HERSKOVITS, 1965, *A Preface to Modern Nigeria.* Madison, Wisc.: University of Wisconsin Press.

An historical account of the freed Yoruba slaves who returned from Sierra Leone and their influence, 1830–1890.

LANDER, RICHARD, 1830, *Records of Captain Clapperton's Last Expedition to Africa,* Vols. I–II. London: Henry Colburn and Richard Bentley.

An account of the earliest known expedition to penetrate Yoruba territory, with a description of Old Ọyọ in Chapters IV and V. See also Clapperton.

LANDER, RICHARD and JOHN, 1832, *Journal of an Expedition to Explore the Course and*

Termination of the Niger. The Family Library, Vols. XXVIII–XXX. London: John Murray.

An account of Richard Lander's return to Old Ọyọ with his brother on the expedition which finally discovered the mouth of the Niger River.

LEIGHTON, ALEXANDER H., T. ADEOYE LAMBO, CHARLES O. HUGHES, DOROTHEA C. LEIGHTON, JANE M. MURPHY, and DAVID B. MACKLIN, 1963, *Psychiatric Disorder among the Yoruba.* Ithaca: Cornell University Press.

An intensive investigation of the subject made by a team of investigators near Abẹokuta in 1961.

LLOYD, P. C., 1962, *Yoruba Land Law.* New York: Oxford University Press.

A survey of the subject based on government files and fieldwork from 1956 to 1959, with special emphasis on Ondo, Ijẹbu, Ado Ekiti, and Ẹgba.

LLOYD, P. C., 1965, "The Yoruba of Nigeria" in James L. Gibbs, Jr. (Ed.), *Peoples of Africa.* New York: Holt, Rinehart and Winston.

A brief (twenty-one pages), general description of the Yoruba, with special emphasis on Ado Ekiti.

OJO, G. J. AFOLABI, 1966, *Yoruba Palaces.* London: University of London Press.

A study of the structure and changes in form of the palaces of Yoruba kings, illustrated with photographs and floor plans.

OJO, G. J. AFOLABI, 1967, *Yoruba Culture.* London: University of London Press.

A geographical analysis of Yoruba culture.

OREWA, G. OKA, 1962, *Taxation in Western Nigeria.* Nigerian Social and Economic Studies No. 4. New York: Oxford University Press.

An analysis of the practices and problems of direct taxation in the Western Region of Nigeria.

PARRINDER, E. G., 1956, *The Story of Ketu.* Ibadan: Ibadan University Press.

An account of the history of the kingdom of Ketu from the founding of its capital to 1956.

SCHATZ, SAYRE P., 1964, *Development Bank Lending in Nigeria.* New York: Oxford University Press.

A study of the Federal Loans Board and its procedures.

TURNER, H. W., 1967, *African Independent Church,* Vols. I–II. New York: Oxford University Press.

An historical account of the origin and spread of the Aladura Church.

WARD, EDWARD, 1938, *The Yoruba Husband–Wife Code.* Washington, D.C.: The Catholic University of America, Anthropological Series No. 6.

A missionary account of marriage and the family in Ondo, with special emphasis on the reciprocal obligations between husbands and wives.

WEBSTER, JAMES BERTIN, 1964, *The African Churches among the Yoruba, 1888–1892.* New York: Oxford University Press.

An historical study of the separatist church movement among the Yoruba.

WILLETT, FRANK, 1967, *Ife in the History of West African Sculpture.* London: Thames and Hudson.

A beautifully illustrated account of the antiquities of Ife's classical period.